Contents

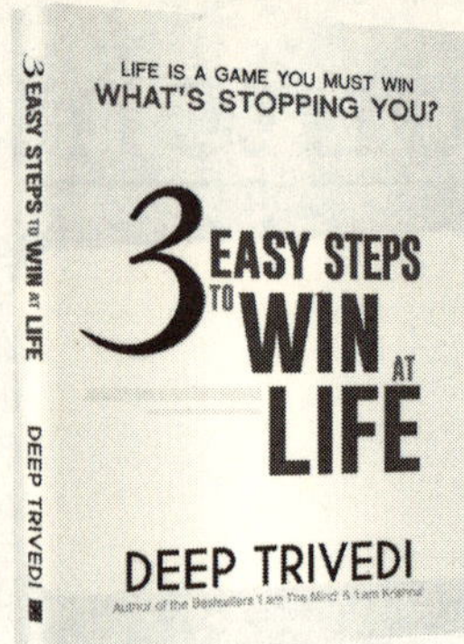

Second Edition: 2022
Price: Rs 349/-

Printed in India

Concept, Illustration and Design:

www.aatmaninnovations.com

Publisher: Aatman Innovations Pvt. Ltd.
Place of Publication: Mumbai

ISBN 978-93-84850-58-6

DEEP TRIVEDI

Deep Trivedi is a renowned author, speaker and pioneer in spiritual psychodynamics. He writes and conducts lectures as well as workshops with an all-pervasive perspective, guiding individuals towards the achievement of their full potential. To date, he has led millions of people onto the path of success and happiness through his works.

In his voluminous works, Deep Trivedi has extensively explained Nature, its laws, its behaviour, its psychology and the effect it has on human life. No aspect of life and human psychology has been left untouched by him. He states that lack of psychological knowledge and understanding is the sole reason for all the sorrows and failures that pervade human life.

He has authored the bestsellers 'I am The Mind', 'I am Krishna' and many more. His bestseller 'I am The Mind' has been published in several national and international languages. He has been awarded the Times Power Men Award 2018 for his immense contribution to society.

His command over the biggest psychologies of life can be gauged by the fact that he holds the record for 'Maximum Lectures on Human Life', 'Maximum Lectures on Psychological Aspects of Tao Te Ching', 'Maximum Lectures on Ashtavakra Gita' and 'Maximum Lectures on Bhagavad Gita', spanning 168 hours, 28 minutes, 50 seconds in 58 days in different National and International record books. He also holds the record for 'Maximum Number of Quotations on Human Life' (about 12038) on subjects such as Soul, Human Life, Psychology, Laws of Nature, Destiny and many more. He has also been awarded an Honorary Doctorate for his Psychological works on the Bhagavad Gita. His interactive workshops have brought about a revolutionary transformation in people's lives by addressing their day-to-day concerns. These lectures and workshops have been delivered in front of live audiences across India.

He is known for his special ability to touch upon the deepest aspects of life and explain them by using lucid language, leaving no scope for ambiguity. The distinct spiritual-psychological language and expression in his writings, lectures and workshops, begin to have an instant effect on the mind of the reader or listener, which makes Deep Trivedi a pioneer in this field.

To know more about Deep Trivedi, visit www.deeptrivedi.com

DEEP TRIVEDI

The Speaker

Deep Trivedi uses a unique combination of psycho-spiritual content, voice, language and expression, which effectuates an instantaneous transformation in his viewers and listeners. Millions of lives have been transformed just by listening to him.

His interactive workshops have brought about a revolutionary transformation in people's lives by addressing their day-to-day concerns. Deep Trivedi sheds light on every aspect of human life and mind and he has extensively spoken on The Bhagavad Gita, Tao Te Ching, Ashtavakra Gita, Secrets of Nature, Mind, Soul, Time, Destiny, and numerous other topics such as:

- **Ego**
- **God**
- **Guilt**
- **Love**
- **Anger**
- **Future**
- **Wealth**
- **Phobias**
- **Religion**
- **Complex**
- **Marriage**
- **Freedom**
- **Partiality**
- **Day-Sleep**
- **DNA-Genes**
- **Path of Life**
- **Personality**
- **Expectation**
- **Acceptance**
- **Hypocrisy**
- **Creativity**
- **Confusion**
- **Good-Bad**
- **Involvement**
- **Concentration**
- **Laws of Nature**
- **Time and Space**
- **Mind and Brain**
- **Self-Confidence**
- **Joy and Happiness**
- **Natural Intelligence**
- **Power of Transformation**

LIFE IS A GAME YOU MUST WIN

WHAT'S STOPPING YOU?

3 EASY STEPS TO WIN AT LIFE

DEEP TRIVEDI

Author of the Bestsellers 'I am The Mind' & 'I am Krishna'

Also available in Hindi, Marathi and Gujarati

Contents

BECOME YOUR OWN LIGHT

At the outset, before we embark on this voyage of self-discovery, you must answer a fundamental question, 'What is it that man values the most?' Beyond a doubt, his life. Rightly so, as every human being is wholeheartedly devoted to his life, leaving no stone unturned in order to prosper and progress. But then, is his life thriving and flourishing as a result? Certainly not! Despite employing all means and methods to make headway in life, for some, life remains a mystery, while for others, a great complexity. Everyone is vexed and troubled in pursuit of the elusive, chasing after something. And when asked for the reason behind such anxiety and restiveness, each person is quick to place the blame on some situation or person. However, this blame game is not a solution, for it is certainly not ousting life's problems and complexities. This brings us to the question, is this all there is to life? Can one not be blithe and merry and lead a serene and successful existence? Indubitably, one can, and history stands witness to many people who have led such lives, leading by example. In fact, even today, tens of thousands of people are verily leading such wonderful lives. This begs the question, then why is the greater part of mankind compelled to lead deplorable lives? This question, in turn, invites another, namely, how are some people able to lead happy and joyous lives with impeccable ease? Why is there a stark difference between two lives? Here, you must comprehend clearly and categorically that the difference lies not in their lives, but in the architect of those lives. The fault lies not with life, but with the one who is directing and manoeuvring it. And pray tell me, who is directing a human being's life? Certainly, a human being is himself steering the course of his life in the direction he wishes to. He is himself making the myriad of decisions, namely, what he must do and not do, in order to render his life successful, and these decisions, in turn, are shaping up his life. This is a simple math that I am certain everyone must have grasped. In essence, this apparent difference of success-failure in everyone's life, is the outcome of the decisions a human being himself has made.

Having said that, if everything in life hinges entirely on its architect, that is to say, upon a human being himself, let us delve deeper and comprehend the human being at some length. For, a human being is in himself a unique being; every individual has a different approach towards undertaking tasks, and the foundation on which people base their decisions also differs from person to person. This is precisely the reason man is inadvertently perplexed and confounded, always mired in confusions wondering, 'Who is following the right course of action, him or others?' And in order to ascertain this, everyone's attention is inevitably focused on other people, trying to comprehend, who is performing the right actions and who is not? They are all constantly engaged in deciphering which actions are right and which are not, for ultimately, they all want to do what is right and set their life on the path of progress. Despite this, nobody can state with conviction as to what is right or what is wrong. For, the thinking process and the manner in which every human being conducts himself varies drastically, which in turn gives rise to delusions. Consequently, every human being perpetually remains in a state of confusion and uncertainty with regard to the actions he undertakes. He is wracked by feelings of regret regardless of him performing an action or refraining from it. And this is why everyone perpetually vacillates between undertaking an action and refraining from it. And interestingly, one is chided not just when one undertakes an action, but even when one doesn't. Alas! What is one supposed to do in such a situation? How should one set one's life on the path of prosperity and progress? To add to the woes, millions of books, scores of communities and thousands of advisors are eager to lend their unsolicited advice to such bewildered people. And the irony is, caught in a conundrum, these confused people then resort to making the rounds of such places, in a bid to seek advice and guidance. For, even though one is confused, one still has to progress in life...even if it is achieved by following other people's advice. In other words, a self-reliant human being, capable of making his own decisions during the initial stage of his life, is reduced to a nervous wreck and ends up depending on the counsel of other people. And this dependency, in turn, gives rise to a new predicament. For, the counsel offered by people of different faiths and communities are at variance with each other, and so are the advice and teachings proffered by different people and books. And eventually, man, who sets out to oust confusions from his life, is further ensnared in their web. Instead of finally setting himself on the path, straight and true, he goes further adrift. And if you were to look around carefully, you would find the majority of human beings languishing in this state.

This begs the question, what recourse must one take in such a case? The answer is simple; one must do that which is in accordance with Nature's design, and follow the methods employed by great people through the ages. For, it is obvious that a confused person cannot get far in life. Moreover, it is a fact that the more advice a person seeks, the more deluded he will be. And one need not go far to substantiate this fact. Simply cast a glance around you; you will notice that the vast majority of people are verily dependent on religion, scriptures, advisors, thinkers and motivational speakers for guidance. And ironically, these very people who offer guidance are the ones deluded with respect to life, and also far more beleaguered with life's problems and vexations. Well, you may wonder, 'In that case, what recourse is one left with?' Well, as stated earlier, one must act in accordance with Nature's design. This, in turn, might prompt you to ask, 'Agreed, but what exactly do you mean by Nature's design?' My friend, be patient; firstly, know well that Nature's design cannot be explained in a single sentence. As the subject is crucial, I will have to establish its foundation in depth. So, first, answer me, who, according to you, should make life's decisions, i.e. who should be considered the ultimate authority with respect to decision-making? Should it be parents, elders, wise men, religion, scholars, teachers, scriptures, thinkers, intelligent people, motivational speakers? Wait! Do not be in a rush to respond... take your time and ponder over this question. If you wish, take a half-hour break at this point. Reflect over this question in peace and solitude, for, everything in life hinges upon the answer to this question.

In answer to the above question, some of you must have ticked two categories from the above-mentioned list, some four and some might have ticked them all. In fact, the majority of you must have even heeded the advice of all the above-mentioned people many times in your life. And all of them must have indubitably influenced your decisions at some point in life. That being the case, just ponder, have you prospered and progressed in life, having secured their guidance? Certainly not! Do you know why? Because, the advice doled out by these people is incongruent with Nature. Funnily enough, these people are always eager to provide guidance, which more often than not is unsolicited advice. Why, even you are no less desperate to obtain their counsel! That is why, you inevitably cross paths with such people at some point or the other. And to corroborate this fact, just look around you; today, the majority of people in the world are verily under the influence of one of these categories. Indeed, how comforting it is to know that man is not solitary and friendless in the game of life! He has an army of 'experts' in tow to render him assistance in his pursuit of progress and prosperity. What splendid news indeed! But then, pray tell me, why are the majority of people not able to attain progress or prosperity in life? Why does everybody find themselves invariably ensnared in some problem or the other? Once you seek the answer to this question, finding the right direction in life will become easier for you. And if you are still unable to grasp it, then I am here, of course, to help you. All in all, this entire kerfuffle is itself against the laws of Nature. The idea of devising numerous avenues for knowledge and dispensing scores of suggestions and advice, is verily against the ultimate principles of psychology. And how can anything positive in life ever be achieved by going against the laws of Nature and the principles of psychology? It is simply impossible! Even so, the greater part of mankind is doggedly striving in a direction that is contrary to Nature and psychology, and this is why such people are mired in problems.

Yes, yes, I can hear your plaintive cry, 'Why don't you come to the point rather than beat around the bush? Why do you not simply tell us, where are we faltering?' I will certainly answer this question, but first let me establish a foundation to what I am about to expound. At the outset, let me explain how man is seeking guidance from this huge army of 'experts' in order to lead his life on the path of progress. Moreover, the quest for such guidance is not a new phenomenon; man has been engaged in this exercise since time immemorial. Even so, life has confounded him for centuries on end, as it continues to be hounded by troubles and difficulties. Curiously, despite this, nobody takes a pause to think over or deliberate upon this state of affairs. No person ever questions or becomes sceptical of the people who proffer such advice and suggestions. No one questions whether they are really in need of these advisors in order to set their life on the path of progress? Despite experiencing a slew of setbacks and failures, everybody remains persistently engaged in their endeavour to make progress in life, with a battery of advisors in tow. Man does not take a lesson from his own undoing or from anybody else's, but instead keeps on scuttling back to these so-called expert guides over and over again. And this is precisely what I object to, for, this is certainly not how great people have led or lead their lives.

I can see you are impatient to ask, *'Now, it is high time that you apprise us of what great people do. Pray tell us, where we are going wrong. Admittedly, we are all endeavouring to set our lives on the path of progress and prosperity with the aid of expert guides and their counsel, but it is not leading us to the life we so seek. Where is it that we are all faltering? What should we do now? Please extricate us out of this problem and guide us onto the right path. How do we prosper and progress? What is it that great people do? Kindly enlighten us with Nature's design and the psychological principle for steering one's life on the path of progress?'*

Ah, now, that's better! Perhaps, I have succeeded in shaking you out of the rut. For, before coming to the point, I earnestly wanted to drive home the point that man is not able to progress in life relying on the counsel of these 'expert guides'. On the contrary, their 'advice' is setting your life even more adrift; instead of abating, life's confusions and perplexities are escalating. Well, this is bound to happen, because coercive advisors have no place in Nature's scheme of things. Besides, seeking guidance from others, time and again, is incongruous with the principles of psychology. And it was precisely to explain this law that I was emphasising on the futility of such expert guides. This subject is indeed profound, so you must comprehend it in all its depth. Hence, before proceeding further, tell me, who, according to you, should be the one taking decisions? You will undoubtedly answer, someone vested with authority. To illustrate this with a simple example, tell me, who makes decisions in a royal court? Certainly, the king, you will say. Ministers, associates and advisors too are in attendance at the royal court, but they go no further than lending their opinion. The authority to take the final decision rests with the king as per his discretion. Now, pray tell me, who is the king of your life? Assuredly, you yourself. Who then are all these advisors that you run to? Beyond a doubt, your courtiers. Now, if they are courtiers, it follows that they can only provide suggestions, and that too, only when asked. However, in actual life, everything has turned upside down; all these external courtiers have been overpowering you. You have allowed them to prevail over you to the extent that now, it has become their wont to directly announce your life's decisions to you. Just think about it, religion decrees who you are and what your identity is, while your parents apprise you of your caste and status. Religious scriptures and texts instruct you when you should visit religious shrines and what you should do at these places. As for the society, it hands you a manual for code of conduct, dictating how to behave, in which place, at what time, where to laugh and where not to, and even how much to laugh. Dieticians are determining your diet, while your parents and guardians are charting the course of your future. Now, just take a moment to ponder over the state of a kingdom, wherein the courtiers pronounce their own decisions, while the king sits helplessly, mute and dumb. You know the answer – it can only be ruin and chaos. So, why do you not realise that allowing others to overpower you has led you to ruination. I am sure you would have grasped this point with the example stated above.

Now, let us grasp the same point with the aid of Nature's design. In Nature's scheme of things, all the decision-making powers should verily be vested with the king; therefore, it follows that the decision should be made by the king alone. That being the case, tell me, who is the king and master of your life? Who is the ultimate authority of your life? Do not, in your overenthusiasm, be eager to spout a careless answer; instead, reflect on it in peace and solitude. If needed, read the above questions over and over again, and weigh them on the scales of the reality of your life. Sit in solitude to reflect over them in depth and ascertain who the master of your life is. Come, let me help you! Sit in solitude and contemplate over each name one by one; reflect, whether it is your parents who are the masters of your life. When you have found the answer to this question, ponder over another question; are your teachers the masters of your life? Once you have arrived at an answer, mull over the next question – Is your life governed by societal dictate? Is your spouse the master of your life? Is it religious scriptures? Is it God? Your endeavour must be to ascertain, how many from the above-mentioned, in your view, are the masters of your life? And here, it is important to be absolutely clear about the meaning of a master. Master, in this context, implies all the people whose presence, instructions, orders and thoughts influence your decisions; in other words, all those who influence your decisions, invariably assume the role of the masters of your life. Now, taking into consideration all the above-mentioned points, tell me, how many masters do you have in life? Answer this question truthfully, because your entire life hinges on the correct assessment of this question. And the correct estimation is, the majority of the above-mentioned people are masters, by and large, for everyone. If assessed correctly, only a smattering of people will be able to assertively state that they have just a few masters, while those who can proclaim that none of the above are their masters will be next to none.

The next question you must ask yourself is, who is really the master of your life? As per Nature's design, the master is the one in whom the authority to make the ultimate decision rests. And who has the ultimate authority over your life? Again, do not rush to answer, take your time to deliberate over this question. Once ready, perhaps, your answer will be, Destiny and God. Assuredly, when I asked you about the ultimate authority in your life, you would have ruled out everything petty and trivial. This brings us to the question, are Destiny and God really the masters of your life? Do they have the power to take the final decisions in your life? Before you strain your brain over it, let me simplify this question. Answer me, whom do you consider God? You will respond, Krishna, Christ, Buddha and their ilk. Fine! So, let us seek the answer to this question by peeping into the lives of these very people! It is common knowledge that Jesus Christ was crucified while he was well alive and breathing. In that case, who do you think had taken the crucial decision of putting him to death, Jesus Christ himself or the people who crucified him? Indubitably, the people who crucified him had taken this decision. In other words, even when Christ was well alive and present before these people, they did not pay heed to his words! What does this imply? This simply implies that the people who slayed Christ had the ultimate authority over their actions; this power was not vested with Christ. In other words, they were their own masters, not Christ. So, when Christ was nobody's master even while he was alive, how can he be your master today? And he obviously is not! This leads us to the conclusion that as per the ultimate design of Nature, every person in this world is his own master.

We shall now comprehend the same point with an example from Krishna's life. It is no secret that Krishna wanted Arjuna to fight the Mahabharata war and not flee from it. And in order to convince him to fight, Krishna enunciated the Bhagavad Gita. During the course of the Gita, Krishna must have urged Arjuna scores of times to arm himself and prepare to fight. But Arjuna simply refused to budge from his decision to not fight, and Krishna, left with no choice, had to perforce stretch the Gita till 700 maxims, enunciating the entire 18 chapters! This eventually goes on to prove that even when Krishna was well and truly alive, it was Arjuna who had the ultimate authority over his own life, not Krishna. So, just ponder, how can Krishna have any authority over your life today? He does not have and neither does he wish to have even a smidgen of authority over you.

Now, the million-dollar question is, when even great beings such as Krishna and Christ do not have any authority over your life, how did a multitude of sundry people become the masters of your life? This also prods us to reflect, why do great beings like Krishna and Christ not have an authority over other people's lives? Both these questions are significant in their import. So, reflect deeply upon them first, and I will then apprise you of the answer. If possible, do not read beyond this point for at least half an hour. First, try to seek the answer to these questions by delving within. This will augment your contemplation power, and if you find the right answers to these questions, it will also serve as a proof that your consciousness is awakened. Now, the answer to the first question—*how do wise men like Christ and Krishna not have even a smidgen of authority over ordinary human beings...?*—is that this is verily Nature's design; in Nature's scheme of things, every human being is his one and only master. Nobody has the authority to make decisions pertaining to others' lives, and as a matter of fact, this verily is the dignity Nature has accorded to every human being. And for this very reason, a human being is the ultimate and finest creation of Nature. Others can exert force on your body, but in no way can they do so with your mind. Your body can be taken prisoner, but not your mind. Your body can be forced to fold hands and greet someone, but nobody has the power to coerce your mind to do the same. And this power is verily your dignity and pride as a human being. And only when you recognise your dignity as a human being, will you be able to proceed on the journey ahead. I am certain, with this elucidation, everybody must have grasped well that they themselves are the sole masters of their lives.

Now, if every person is the sole master of his life, the question arises—how did so many people assume command and become the masters of your life? How on earth is any Tom, Dick and Harry able to control and prevail over you? Now, once again, it is you who must first try to find the answer to this question yourself, because doing so will enhance your thinking power. And augmentation of one's thinking power is pivotal to set one's life on the path of progress. However, let me give you a hint to make it easier for you. To decipher any matter pertaining to psychology, go on retracing your steps, one step at a time. This gradual but consistent retrospection will help you arrive at the root cause; and this verily is the ultimate principle of psychology. So, put on your thinking cap and try to seek the answer to this question by yourself. Well, now that you have reflected on this question, I shall tell you how your life's ownership is slipping away from your hands. Simply put, you have been losing your ownership on account of the desires you harbour. And that is why, even in the most ancient psychology of religion, 'desire' has been termed as the greatest foe of human beings. As soon as you nurse a wish for something, others gain leverage over you by luring you with the greed of fulfilment of that wish. Be it community, society or businesses, everybody takes advantage of this human weakness, and that is why you have become a puppet in their hands. Your second enemy in this regard is your ego, because prompted by ego, you shroud yourself in beliefs and opinions, which then assume command and seize the reins of your life. Further, your dependencies and expectations open up avenues for others to establish their dominance over you. As a result, your life is reduced to a deplorable state, confined by compulsions and constraints, which in turn, allows other people to gain greater control over your life. Now, I need not elucidate the entire chain of slavery in all its lurid details here, as this is not a book on psychology. I have briefly explained how others gain control over you because of your desires, ego, expectations and dependency, and trusting your sensibilities, a hint should suffice for you.

Interestingly, our discussion so far has helped us realise how other people assume control over our lives. But you might well ask, what difference does it make? After all, they are more prudent and knowledgeable than us. Allowing them to assume the reins of our life is for our betterment, isn't it? Wonderful! That is precisely what I wanted to hear! My friend, the notion that others are more knowledgeable or better than you, is not your own; it is, in fact, drilled into your mind by the people who have gained supremacy over you. This is a formidable, illusory trap to turn men into slaves and plunder them mentally. Such people make you believe that you are not a good person. And you, in turn, with folded hands, ask with utmost humility, "What should I do in order to become a good person?" This one question of yours is enough to turn you into a slave. And then begins the onslaught; you are told that you lack self-confidence and concentration, and ironically, you readily acknowledge the same, without even comprehending what these two attributes mean or what is their psychology. And no sooner you accept the decree announced by others than the shackles of slavery further tighten their grip around you. Likewise, you are told that you are not religious and again, you accept it, without even trying to discern what being religious truly means. And then the trap widens to include everything, right from what you must eat to where you must go. Everything with regard to what you must do and not do in life is explained to you. Sadly, the greater majority of human beings have become trapped in this labyrinth. With this, I have given you a significant hint; so be cautious! As for the rest, I will certainly shed light on what you must do in order to extricate yourself from this trap in the succeeding pages, but prior to that, let me lay down a solid foundation of the book.

So, before we proceed further, another important point that demands contemplation is, why did Nature mandate every person in this world to be the sole master of his life? Well, this is verily the play of life; in Nature's scheme of things, every human being is the master of his life, and he is bound to bear the consequences of his actions as well. In other words, you have to sow yourself and you alone have to reap. You get to relish the reward of your good actions, and you alone will be penalised for your bad deeds as well. Nobody in this world can either receive another's reward or bear the consequences of somebody else's misdeeds. If you have established any such connection, then it is but your delusion. Ingrain what I have just said deep into your mind. I am giving you some really important indications, one after the other, so stay alert and grasp them. Moving further, you must comprehend that since a human being is his sole master in Nature's design, Nature has invariably equipped him with all the powers required to set his life on the path of progress. That is to say, Nature has not been unjust towards mankind even a wee bit. A human being is born equipped with the entire gamut of powers requisite to carve a splendid life for himself. In other words, he is not meant to be dependent on others in order to prosper and progress. But there is a catch here; these powers can be activated only when a human being is the true master of his life. If he becomes servile to a multitude of masters, then the powers that he was born with will remain dormant throughout his life. Such people are then compelled to run to saviours and live at the mercy of so-called advisors and experts. However, this is against the very principles of Nature and is precisely the reason why such people are not able to accomplish much in life. Sorrows, worries, frustration and tension plague their mind, while endless struggle and strife become their inevitable destiny. Now, for my part, I have revealed the ultimate secret of Nature to you; I have made it amply clear that you are the sole master of your life. And only if you continue to remain the master, all your mind's powers and intelligence will automatically be available at your disposal. The dependencies you have assumed in order to prosper and progress in life will vanish, and only then, will it be possible for you to steer your life on the path of happiness, peace, joy and success. This is the first principle established by Nature for human beings, which emphasises that any kind of dependency in this world is an impediment to man's progress. Thus, before we proceed further, comprehend this point well and embed it in your mind. As for the rest, we will certainly discuss and discern everything that is essential with reference to this point.

Hey, don't press ahead! Please do not be in a rush. First, explain to us, in what way are we the ultimate authority in our life? How are we our only master? Please elucidate this in greater detail.

Alright, I shall explain, but before I do, you must answer a couple of questions. Tell me, which person in the world knows everything about you...? That person is verily your master and you must seek advice only from him. So, answer me, who is that person? Do not overthink; that person is you yourself! And this is Nature's design for you whereby you have to answer nobody, save your own self. It is, indeed, Nature's miracle that nobody in this world knows you better than yourself. So, it is imperative for you to comprehend that you alone are your master. And without grasping this truth, nothing of consequence shall ever transpire in your life. To illustrate this point, let me give you an example from your day-to-day life. Tell me, who will be the first to know if you are suffering from a headache? Beyond a doubt, you yourself. Now, can the people whom you consider wise and great, or for that matter, even doctors and scientists, become aware of your headache, unless you apprise them of it or give some sign? Certainly not! This simply implies, whether it is a great person or a doctor, nobody can ever be more aware about you than your own self. Moving further, tell me, who decides what course of action should be taken to mitigate the headache? Again, unquestionably, it is you who decides whether you must pop a pill, visit a doctor or simply wait for the headache to dissipate on its own. In the same vein, it is only you who can tell if the headache still persists or has been cured. In other words, as far as your life is concerned, nobody has greater authority over it than you. You are verily the captain of your ship, one who will navigate it in the right direction.

Interestingly, despite this fact being so evident, a great number of people and objects are still ruling over your life. Why so? Can you provide me with one valid reason for this? It is because, the manner in which you treat your mind or your life differs vastly from how you deal with your body. In case of physical problems, you are aware of it at first, whereas in case of your mind and life, some enlighten you that you are not religious; while others apprise you of your caste and religion. Why, they even determine whether or not you are stylish and if you are confident or otherwise. That is to say, it is not you who has arrived at the conclusion that you are unreligious, unsocial and impractical... it is the world which has displayed its largesse in explaining your shortcomings to you. In other words, where the physical aspect is concerned, you are the first one to realise that you have a headache, while on the mental plane, others become cognisant of your unreligious state even before you do. This is, indeed, remarkable! And not one or two, almost every human being has performed this miraculous feat! And now everyone is part of this mad circus. You seek the refuge of tens of hundreds of people in order to become religious, social and practical. And then you are embroiled in this circus and the resultant drama till the time you breathe your last. If you find this difficult to believe, then once again reflect deeply on your present life, and you will realise that you are a mere puppet, dancing to the tunes orchestrated in a circus owned by somebody else.

Now, pause and take a moment to think, isn't this a deplorable situation? Why, it most certainly is! This is an extremely grave matter, for, in this case, you are disrespecting another conception of Nature, that every human being in this world is unique, novel and one-of-his-kind; nobody like him has ever graced this world before. When no two faces are identical, then the possibility of two minds or lives being alike is simply inconceivable. Even so, in a bid to solicit advice, everybody has taken to imitating each other. Consequently, a crowd of thousands congregates in the same place, for the same reason; and a human being who ought to have been a unique individual with an inimitable personality, has become a faceless part of the milieu. A human being who had to be his own unique self, has become like so many others in the crowd. Now, pray tell me, how can a person, who is completely devoid of individuality, ever amount to much in life? You can observe for yourself, the majority of people, devoid of their individuality, are unable to get far in life. So, kindly etch this in your mind that you have no master save for yourself, and you have to become only like yourself. Only if you apprehend these two points, will you be able to accomplish something in life.

Now, you may be tempted to say, *'Agreed, we are our own masters, and nobody like us has ever been born. We accept that we have to stay true to ourselves. But what difference will it make, even if we do all of this? How will we achieve happiness and progress with the help of this?'*

Well, the answer is, if and only if you truly believe in this and become your own self in the truest sense, will the powers of your mind become activated and you will be able to connect with and tap into Nature's ultimate power. And only then will your life take a turn for the better, else, despite endless labour and toil, you will keep swirling in a whirlpool of sorrows and failures. Why do you not realise that we are mankind, that wonderful offspring of Nature, for whom Nature has laid down its own unique design? And human life can turn into a beautiful experience, only if we honour that design and align with it. If you think human life can prosper and progress by paying heed to superficial words and resorting to nonsensical means, then you are sadly mistaken.

Well, what is done is in the past. But, in the present, what can we do to improve our situation?

Well, going forward, endeavour to righten all the wrongs in order to ensure that at least the remainder of your life is beautiful and glorious. However, this will not become a reality by veering off the path that Nature has chalked out for you. This is, indeed, a crucial point; for, the fact is, as far as Nature is concerned, every human being has only one valuable possession - his 'life'. Ergo, whatever has to occur in one's life will invariably occur in the natural flow of his life. He does not have to resort to any monkey business separately in order to do so, for doing so will alter both life's pace and its natural path. If you are unable to grasp this point, then read the above-mentioned statement repeatedly, for, this is verily the ultimate principle of time and space with respect to human beings. However, presently, we are not discussing profound subjects like time and space; my only objective, at present, is to make your life even more sublime. And to that end, you must comprehend that if you have strayed from the right course in life, then it is only because you have veered off the path Nature had chosen for you. Had you seamlessly flowed along the course of your life, you would have never strayed from your path. Let me illustrate this point with an example. As you are well aware, the greater majority of human beings have faith in one community, creed or sect, and in order to abide by their faith, they also visit their respective religious places such as temples, mosques and churches on a regular basis. They read the scriptures and chant *mantras* as well, because they believe that doing so will enhance their mind and life. But, pray tell me, how many people have succeeded in eradicating miseries and anguish from their lives abiding by their religious code of conduct? How many people were able to rid themselves of jealousy despite practising every virtue prescribed by the scriptures and so-called *gurus*? How many have refrained from inflicting wrong upon others? On the contrary, on a daily basis, a number of so-called holy men are found mired in crime and nefarious activities. For, engaging in the acts that are incongruent with the principles of time and space will only spawn perversions in the mind. Thus, apprehend once and for all that your religion is nothing but your 'life'. And if you wish to uphold your religion, you can do so only by being in sync with the flow of life. Besides, it is not necessary for everyone to subscribe to spirituality or philosophy as a part of their lives. Every human being has his own life and his own path; ergo, kindly forsake the habit of doing anything which makes you stray from the path of your life. This is my earnest advice to you, because I am certain, you are habituated to fulfilling not just your religious obligations, but tens of other commitments too, veering off your life path. Little do you realise that in this process, you hand over the command of your life to everybody else. I hope, you must have grasped my allusion and you will henceforth keep your focus concentrated on the natural flow of your life. You will embrace with open arms, everything you receive in the flow of life while letting go of everything you do not receive.

Since we have broached this topic, let me also reveal the infallible truth that nobody in this world has a right to proffer advice to other people. It really does not matter how knowledgeable the person providing the advice may be; the path or course of action one chooses should invariably be one's independent decision. In fact, cast a glance at the deeds of great men; no great person has ever tried to interfere in the lives of other human beings. History is replete with examples of innumerable great men like Buddha, Krishna, Christ, Lao Tzu and Kabir. All of them have been accorded the stature of God, but have any of them ever urged you to visit temples, mosques or churches? Of course not! It is the egoists who have assayed doing so by penning nonsensical scriptures, and then, these very egoists have also gone on to devise ludicrous social norms for you to abide by. Why do you not comprehend the simple fact that the signal your brain receives pertaining to when and how much to eat can be transmitted by only your stomach, and most importantly, only you will be privy to this information! Neither can anybody else get an inkling of the same nor are they entitled to interfere in this matter; and this applies to all other matters as well. At the most, those who are great, intelligent or wise can offer you guidance; but even they cannot force you to act against your wishes. And as far as you are concerned, you can surely seek guidance from other people; but under no circumstances should you ever give in to the pressure. The final decision should invariably rest with you, and this is verily in your best interest too. In short, welcome guidance from others, try to grasp what they have to say, and even seek advice...but let the final decision rest with you alone. I state this emphatically, for, nobody possesses more knowledge about you than you yourself. Regardless of the situation, always respect this design of Nature, be aligned with it and maintain distance from people who wish to pressurise or force you; in fact, keep them at bay. For my part, I have provided you with a hint; now, it is up to you to grasp it.

Moving along, let us proceed to the question, 'What should the next step be?' Well, if you, indeed, wish to lead a beautiful and magnificent life, then let your life take its natural course right from this very day, this very moment and this very place. Do not try to resort to any other solutions; I will provide you with a few practical applications, which can be carried out while leading your day-to-day life, and all you have to do is put them into practice. If you do so, everything will happen automatically and you will regain authority and control over your life to a great degree. Your inner minds will become active and get into play; your happiness, joy and concentration will soar; your work efficiency will gradually improve and if you persevere, it will be enhanced drastically. And, before you know it, your life will take a turn for the better, and trust me, this will all occur automatically. All you need to do is, grasp every practical application earnestly and thoroughly, imbibe it in the deep recesses of your mind, and endeavour to put it into practice to the best of your ability. This world has always functioned automatically and it will forever function on automation mode. Likewise, the positive impact of these practical applications on your life will also manifest automatically i.e. on its own. For, these applications are neither fantastical nor nonsensical. All these practical applications are being provided to you, bearing in mind Nature's design as well as the principles of psychology. Ergo, these will have a significant, profound and lasting effect on every human being's life. Just go on implementing one practical application after another and the rest will be grasped automatically.

However, before we begin with the practical applications, let me narrate an incident to you from the life of Gautama Buddha, in his own inimitable style, titled 'My Last Words – Buddha'.

My Last Words – Buddha

Believe it or not, I am Buddha, speaking. I recall perfectly well, my health had deteriorated drastically, and I had all but realised that I was breathing my last. My disciple, Ananda, who had stayed by my side for the past twenty-five years, was seated by my bedside, with his brow furrowed in consternation and a deep sadness etched on his face on apprehending the state of my health. For my part, I was dumbfounded to notice the look of distress on his face; of what consequence was the learning he had gained from me all these years, if my probable death was making him so woeful and grief-stricken? I wondered, if the disciple who had lived with me for twenty-five years has not broken free from the shackles of misery and sorrow, what wisdom would the others have imbibed from me?

Interestingly, while I was still trying to come to grips with his miserable state, Ananda's next words left me completely nonplussed. In all earnestness, he asked me, "O Buddha! Grant me a truth that will liberate me forever." Now, had I spoken lies all my life that I would bestow some ultimate truth on my beloved disciple at the time of my death? Besides, who am I to bestow truth upon anybody? I can only show the way; the person has to himself discern the 'truth' and he himself has to attain it. Does a human being have the power to grant or take anything from anyone? Certainly not! So, I answered, "My friend, always bear this in mind – *Appo Deepo Bhava i.e.* be your own light."

Verily, these were my last words and even today, after a period of two thousand and five hundred years, I am offering you the same advice, *Appo Deepo Bhava* or Be Your Own Light. In fact, this is the essence of everything that I have said and done throughout my life. I proclaim with conviction, if you take this message to heart and imbibe it wholly, you will be liberated instantly. I had to show you the way and I have done so; now, it is you who has to tread that path and discover your own truth. I can do no more! Just think, when I was not in a position to do anything for anyone during my lifetime, what can be achieved today by carving my sculptures or emulating my attire? So, free yourself from all such antics and save yourself from becoming deluded. Set off forthwith on the path shown by me and engage yourself in discovering your life's truth. Trust me, you have no other recourse, save for effecting your deliverance yourself. You will simply have to become your own 'light' and illuminate your path.

Well, you read what Buddha had to say. With his words, you must have comprehended that to become one's own light is verily the ultimate knowledge of human life; and all other knowledge is inconsequential in the absence of this knowledge. This is the very reason I assertively state, all your endeavours in which you expect someone else to light up your path, are nothing save for an exercise in absurdity. And the problem is, you are engaged in myriad endeavours wherein some are apprising you of your pain, while others are buoying you up. Whereas, in Nature's scheme of things, you are the patient as well as the doctor. That is precisely why, Buddha is urging you to 'become your own light'. And you have to become your own light, your own doctor in all these practical applications that I am providing you, because nobody is wiser, more knowledgeable or powerful than you, as regards yourself. As far as all these practical applications are concerned, not only are you the patient but it is verily you, who can be cognisant of the illness too, and must, therefore, become your own doctor and heal yourself. This is verily the world's Three-Dimensional Theory for human beings and is the only effective method of setting your life on the path of progress. All these practical applications are devised bearing in mind Nature's design and the principles of psychology. That is why I implore you to simply put these applications into practice, and they will automatically usher ever more positive transformations in your life. Furthermore, all these practical applications are segregated into three steps wherein you can call step 1 your schoolhouse education. If you clear that step, you will gain admission into step 2, which you can term your graduation. And if you pass this step as well, you will become a doctor of the (human) mind and life, and then, Nature will itself honour you with a doctorate. And pray tell, once you have secured Nature's support, who can stop you from attaining 'greatness'? The only person stopping you from attaining greatness is you yourself, swayed as you are by vain and pointless pronouncements. Ergo, become your own doctor, perform a perfect surgery on yourself and establish the foundation to a great life ahead. The world without has always been a madhouse and it will always remain so. Thus, you have no recourse, save to become your own doctor and treat yourself of the maladies that have ensnared you. And verily, I have provided these practical applications in three distinct steps to aid you to become your own doctor. So, without further ado, let us proceed to the practical applications of Step 1.

PRACTICAL APPLICATIONS
STEP 1

A) Root Yourself Firmly in Your Present Life

At the outset, let me ask you a simple question; from where can one commence a journey? Indubitably, from the current location. If you are currently stationed in Delhi and have to travel to New York, from where can your journey possibly begin? Certainly, from Delhi. But when it comes to life, you do not act thus. Propelled by desires, you often take off on flights of fancies wherein although you are currently situated at point A, you plan your journey from an altogether different point B. And while it is certainly possible to indulge in such wishful thinking and imaginary flights of fantasy, it is not practically possible to materialise it. Thus, as a first step, stop harbouring impractical desires and indulging in digressive flights of fancies, and comprehend that if you are present in Delhi, you have no choice but to commence your journey from Delhi itself. Consider this point as the very first lesson of your life. Else, you will be left making grandiose declarations while life will slip away from your hands, and eventually, even getting through a workaday life will seem like a herculean task.

Ergo, comprehend life's first principle clearly and conclusively - Your journey can begin only from the point where you are currently stationed. This engenders the question, who can be called a masterful traveller? Undoubtedly, someone whose limbs are in good shape, who is in robust health, and is lively, spirited and energetic. Similarly, life is akin to a journey, wherein one can progress only if one travels forth, but to that effect, it is first imperative for one to be fit enough. Thus, before deciding to press forward, firmly station yourself where you presently are. For, only then will you be able to make the most of every excursion you undertake in the journey of life. Otherwise, frittering away your life and energies in nonsensical proclamations and pointless exertions will eventually drain you of all your energy and leave you tired and enervated. Thus, do not try to soar high with your head in the clouds; you are living on the ground, so kindly keep your feet rooted to the ground. In short, first and foremost, firmly root yourself in your present life. And in order to ascertain where you are presently stationed, I will guide you by means of the following chart.

List	Examples
Present employment	Study, Job, Business
Your assets	House, car
Your income	1 million
Your family	Parents, wife and two kids
Health	Good
Hobbies	Food, Travel
Friends	Rakesh, Suchita, Anand

List	To be filled by you (in pencil)
Present employment	
Your assets	

Your income
Your family

Health
Hobbies

Friends ....
....
....
....
....
....
....
....
....
....
....
....
....
....

Now, compile a list of these seven points with respect to your present life and thereafter ascertain whether or not, you are thoroughly enjoying your hobbies, your possessions and the time you spend with your friends and family; pay special attention to whether you are doing full justice to them all. And if you are not, then start enjoying these aspects of your life from this day onwards. At the same time, come to terms with your current income, regardless of the figure, with good grace. In other words, accept and root yourself, both mentally as well as physically, wherever you presently find yourself in life. I will give you a month's time, in order to attain this goal. If you wish, you can compile a list of obstacles and present troubles in achieving this goal. For example, let's imagine your present trouble is your income, and the fact that you do not earn much. In that case, will you act stingy and live like a miser, or be content with your income, regardless of its nature and volume, and start making the most of your life? Pray tell me, what difference does the size of your car make, if it is in good working condition and serves your purpose? If your life partner pesters you with a barrage of questions, either emphatically ask them to hold their tongue or continue to answer them. But establish yourself firmly wherever you are stationed at present; I simply do not want to see you carrying the burden of these troubles a month from now. In other words, improve the areas wherever possible and reconcile yourself mentally to matters which are beyond your control and where no remedial action is possible. But, no matter what, become settled in your current life, and settle in such a way that even if your life continues in the exact same groove till your last breath, you can proudly declare without an iota of remorse – *My life is, indeed, delightful*. And once you become the proud master of such a happy-go-lucky life, know that you are now completely fit to undertake the journey ahead, prepared to face all the curveballs that life may throw at you in the future. Believe me, once you achieve this mindset, nobody can stop you from emerging victorious in the game of life. For, this achievement implies, you are psychologically set for a grand journey ahead. Do you know, what is the speciality of psychology? Perhaps, you don't, so let me answer it for you. Psychology is another term for pressing the button at point A to usher an outcome at point B. In common parlance, I have asked you to become firmly settled in your present life and be content with whatever you have, regardless of its amount and value. I have asked you to reconcile yourself with irremediable circumstances and possessions in life. Now, being content with everything you have at present might seem like a loss-making proposition to the ones who are desperate; they may surmise this as missing the boat or the chance to advance in life. But they are verily mistaken. Psychology works like magic; it is a power that elevates the human might to unimaginable heights. So remarkable are the switches of psychology that when one presses the button at one point, it results in an explosion at an altogether different point. But sadly, there is a dearth of profound psychological knowledge in this world even today. Now, although you have perused through everything I have stated so far, you will gain clarity in this regard only once you comprehend the outcome I wish to bring about with this step. If you, indeed, wish to learn and comprehend psychology, do not read beyond this point for an hour or so. First, sit in solitude and experience settling yourself in your current life. If you really accomplish this, then all the outcomes I desire for you will start reflecting within you. Firstly, write down what you are experiencing within upon getting settled in your present life, and thereafter, read the list of outcomes I have provided. If both are in agreement, then know that your psychological power has begun to amplify. And, once and for all, grasp that there is no power greater and more effective for a human being than psychological knowledge.

Simultaneously, reflect on the psychological change manifesting in your life once you have completely settled yourself in your present life. For, I wish to set your mind by bidding you to do so; I wish to bring a few changes within you on the strength of which you can set off on the journey of progress and prosperity with full might and vigour. Thus, without further ado, observe your state of mind once you have settled in your present life, and cross-check it with the following list of outcomes.

1) You will experience an instant mitigation in sorrows, tensions and frictions in your life, because you have come to terms with everything that exists in every facet of your life at present.
2) You will learn to avoid and let go of everything that is trifling and inconsequential.
3) You will experience a surge in energy and happiness.
4) Increased energy and reduced stress will enable you to accomplish tasks more efficiently and effectively. In other words, your work performance will improve and this, in turn, will open the floodgates to prosperity and progress.
5) You will stop engaging in futile pursuits. Consequently, you will be liberated from unnecessary losses and tensions.
6) Never again will you be faced with the possibility of regressing in life.
7) You will be able to give your 100 per cent and do full justice not only to your friends and family but also to your hobbies and interests.

8) Most importantly, you will always be filled with fervour and vitality, ready to march ahead. In other words, as soon as the opportunity strikes, you will be able to utilise it optimally, and this will boost your chances of making a giant leap in life almost overnight. Else, riddled with constant worries pertaining to the future and running helter-skelter propelled by numerous futile desires, you will turn into a sad, forlorn and enervated person. And such a wearied and beaten person is unable to accomplish anything of great consequence even when an opportunity knocks on his door. Crushed by the burden of familial strain or stress at work, his entire life gets squandered in vain pursuits.

I am certain that with the above discussion, you must have comprehended the multi-pronged attacks of psychology. You would have discerned psychology's speciality of focusing at point A, while aiming at point B. And, certainly, you must have also fully comprehended the importance of being firmly settled and rooted in your present life, without harbouring illusions of any kind. If you have still not grasped this fact, comprehend clearly once again that you cannot make great strides in life unless you invoke your inner power to the best of your capacity and be settled in your present life. And even if perchance, you advance a step or two without having settled yourself firmly, you will have to endure endless difficulties and bear multiple losses. Ergo, I will give you a month's time; get completely settled in your present life, once and for all. With grace and gratitude, accept whatever you have in your present life and make peace with it. Enjoy the present to the fullest and fling open the doors for future success. For, the journey will invariably begin from the point where you are stationed at present, and that too, once you are ready with full determination and an absolutely fresh mind.

Come, let me apprise you of another easy method of becoming firmly grounded and settled in your present life. Actually, I have already discussed this earlier, but let me make it simpler for you to comprehend, with the aid of a chart.

1 Problem

Can you dispel the problem or
will you have to reconcile with it?

☐ **Can be dispelled** ☐ **Will have to reconcile with it**

If it can be dispelled, then put a tick (✔) after doing so
If you have to reconcile with it put a tick (✔) accordingly

☐ **Problem dispelled** ☐ **Reconciled with it**

2 Problem

Can you dispel the problem or
will you have to reconcile with it?

☐ **Can be dispelled** ☐ **Will have to reconcile with it**

If it can be dispelled, then put a tick (✔) after doing so
If you have to reconcile with it put a tick (✔) accordingly

☐ **Problem dispelled** ☐ **Reconciled with it**

3 Problem

Can you dispel the problem or
will you have to reconcile with it?

☐ **Can be dispelled** ☐ **Will have to reconcile with it**

If it can be dispelled, then put a tick (✔) after doing so
If you have to reconcile with it put a tick (✔) accordingly

☐ **Problem dispelled** ☐ **Reconciled with it**

4 Problem

Can you dispel the problem or will you have to reconcile with it?

☐ **Can be dispelled** ☐ **Will have to reconcile with it**

If it can be dispelled, then put a tick (✔) after doing so
If you have to reconcile with it put a tick (✔) accordingly

☐ **Problem dispelled** ☐ **Reconciled with it**

5 **Problem**

Can you dispel the problem or will you have to reconcile with it?

☐ **Can be dispelled** ☐ **Will have to reconcile with it**

If it can be dispelled, then put a tick (✔) after doing so
If you have to reconcile with it put a tick (✔) accordingly

☐ **Problem dispelled** ☐ **Reconciled with it**

I have provided you with this chart so that you can fill it up in this book itself. Know that it is verily these troubles which are acting as an impediment in your path to root yourself in your present life. So, without further ado, expel those impediments one by one; and if the trouble cannot be eliminated, make peace with it and live your life accepting it without an iota of hesitation. Accept wholeheartedly that this trouble is an inevitable part of your present life; desensitise your mind temporarily and bear that trouble at least for the present. Perhaps, things may change in the future. But, for the present, make sure that you either solve your troubles or accept them and live in harmony with them. Keep a track of the progress you have made in resolving your problems, and put a tick against those which you have resolved and also against those with which you have reconciled yourself. And the day all your troubles vanish, know that you have become settled in your present life. Once you make peace with the current state of your life, take note of the positive psychological impacts that I have listed earlier. If you can feel those effects in your life, then apprehend that the aircraft of your life is poised to take off on a magnificent flight soon. And, the bonus is, you no longer have to live a sorrow-stricken life in the present either; you get to lead a happy and fulfilled life even in the present.

On this note, comprehend another law of Nature - Nothing in this world manifests out of nowhere; it is our own doing or undoing that shapes up our life. Every human being thinks, 'Let me first accomplish all the tasks on my to-do list, attain everything I desire, and only then will I settle with an air of contentment.' Caught in the rat race, everyone is embroiled in this mindless struggle, and consequently, unable to settle in life. For, Nature's law is simple - the one who is treading on shaky grounds today, will always remain unsettled. In other words, the one who is not settled or content today will never be settled or content in the future. Thus, if you truly wish to lead your life blithely and merrily, then it is imperative to firmly settle yourself in your present life. For, only then will you be able to exercise considerable control over your life. Why don't you realise that you are upset only because you no longer have authority over your life? So, to get settled and be content in every conceivable way in your present life is the first step towards achieving progress. I am sanguine that you must have comprehended the significance of this crucial step, and that you will settle yourself in your present life in a month's time. Resolve that you will transform yourself into a wonderful, happy-go-lucky person, abounding with vim and vitality.

B) Know Yourself Inside Out

Now, let's take our discussion further to the second application in Step 1, which entails knowing yourself in and out. You must fathom well and truly, what kind of a person you are and what is your psychology. This verily is the second application that will help you anchor yourself firmly in Step 1. To aid you in this exercise, I am providing you with a chart for your convenience. Please do not be in a rush to fill it up; wait until you have really comprehended your true inner self. Whatever happens, do not let this opportunity to know yourself, go in vain.

Do you keep things to yourself or are you expressive? In other words, do you express whatever is going on in your mind?

....

....

....

....

....

....

....

....

....

....

....

Are you talkative or reserved?

Is your manner of speaking impressive or ordinary?

Are you bold and outspoken or shy?

Do you prefer solitude or are you fond of company?

Are you sober or playful?

Is your personality ordinary or impressive?

Do you consider yourself talented or average?

Are you able to make friends easily?

Do your relationships last or come undone for the slightest of reasons?

Once again, I reiterate, do not be in a rush to fill out this chart; do it at your own pace when your mind is at peace, for you need to pen your thoughts with utmost care, after giving it due consideration. And once you have finished, sit back and ponder over what you have written. Then contemplate deeply on whether you consider any of these as your weaknesses. The reason I have asked you to engage in this exercise is to create awareness within you; for instance, in case you are not good at speaking or are unable to express yourself well, do you perceive it as your weakness? If you do consider it your weakness, then you are, indeed, committing a grave mistake. This world is home to a variety of people, and you are a unique person in your own right. So, being unable to speak well has nothing to do with being weak or being at a disadvantage; the only point that really matters is that you must be able to discern yourself in entirety. For, till the time you do not know yourself, how do you expect to deal with the world? Why don't you comprehend the simple fact that in order to drive a car, you must be well versed with the car's mechanism; in the same vein, in order to drive the automobile of your life successfully, you must be aware and well versed with every aspect of yourself; i.e. you must know yourself inside out. You must be able to state with conviction, "This is who I am! And regardless of how I am, I am definitely not weak." For, if you believe there is a shortcoming in you, you will attempt to change yourself, and from that very instant, you will fall prey to exploitation. People will subjugate you and assume control over your life under the pretext of bringing about a change in you. And a shortcoming, in its truest sense, is to allow others to snatch away the reins of your life from you. Ergo, I am warning you, do not let this happen. Accept yourself just the way you are, by believing that you are perfect. Neither make attempts to change yourself nor try to fix yourself in any way. The world is teeming with selfish and manipulative people, who will relentlessly point out your shortcomings for their own selfish gains. They will inevitably find faults with you for no reason, but you must simply disregard it all and turn a blind eye to it. Retain and safeguard your individuality and do not ever try to change yourself in any way, else you will be a sitting duck for exploitation. Besides, comprehend clearly that the world abounds with all kinds of human beings. So, did greatness elude those who were reserved in speech? Not at all! Scores of people who were introverts have attained greatness, and history bears witness to this fact. Have those who were unable to express themselves well, not become great? Of course, they have succeeded in leaving their imprints in this world. There are multitudes with subdued personalities who have attained the peaks of success, and at the same time, the wild and wilful ones have also made a name for themselves. So, there is absolutely no need to worry; just recognise and know yourself well and truly. Believe that you are perfect, irrespective of your nature and personality. And if you are perfect, there is no need to change, and when there is no need to change, there is no scope for exploitation either.

Besides, as far as change is concerned, you will not even realise when and to what extent, you will change automatically while treading life's natural course. Many a time, you must have also observed, the ones who were wild and wilful turning into calm and sober personalities, and people with reserved personalities becoming boisterous and unruly with the passage of time. This change, however, occurs naturally, while treading life's path. Your mind is aware of the necessities of your life and it will automatically change, wisening under the fire of life's experiences, at the right time and to the right extent. This, indubitably, is the best process wherein the mind seamlessly ushers in the change in itself. Hence, do not try to change yourself forcibly; knowing yourself inside out is sufficient in order to make strides in life. Indeed, there is no need for you to expose yourself to the world in a bid to effect a change in yourself. I hope you will accomplish this task with ease, for knowing oneself inside out plays a major role in helping one lead a life abounding in happiness and prosperity.

Besides, I have already elucidated the multi-pronged attack of psychology, wherein the switch is flicked at point A to trigger an outcome at point B. Focusing at one point while targeting the other is psychology's peculiarity. So, while I am asking you to comprehend yourself, I am, in fact, transforming you into a confident human being.

As soon as you discern yourself and accept yourself just the way you are, and subsequently let go of the desire to change, you will immediately start abounding with peace, tranquillity and merriment. You will be infused with immense confidence in carrying out life's functions. And, believe me, this is no mean feat; for, this will boost your energy, thus, enhancing your inclination towards work. Moreover, your heightened confidence with respect to life will automatically set you on the path of success. And trust me, you will score these achievements so effortlessly that you will be surprised yourself! As opposed to this, you might labour and toil your utmost in any other field, but you will fail to garner this kind of achievement. You might even spend copious amounts of money, but it will all be in vain. For, somebody else will be the doctor in that case, whereas the fact of the matter is, you have to become your own doctor and treat your own self. And that is precisely why I am making you, your own doctor and your own master. For, this is verily Nature's design for you and herein lies your betterment. Moreover, this is the only solution which will beget results. Ergo, become your own doctor and recognise who you are, well and truly. Once you have comprehended who you are, accept yourself in entirety. And once you have discerned yourself thoroughly, it won't be long before you transform into a remarkable personality. And these changes will take place speedily, simultaneously and automatically. For that matter, only changes that take place speedily, simultaneously and automatically prove to be of consequence. For, one's lifespan is not long, after all! In a life that is but fleeting, how can one wait and sit around for a positive change to occur? So, I hope, you will immediately effect this great transformation within yourself.

C) Identify Your Strengths and Weaknesses

Ideally, you should have a full reckoning of your strengths and weaknesses, because all these strengths and weaknesses are for your self-assessment. You must determine them on your own, and you must do so for your own sake. The world has no role to play whatsoever in this exercise. Bear in mind, your strengths and weaknesses should be adjudged by none but yourself; under no circumstances should they be surmised by other people. After all, it is you who has to become your own doctor. So, deliberate upon your strengths and weaknesses carefully. For, the game of life is plain and simple; your strengths will accrue you rewards, while you will have to pay (through your nose) for your weaknesses. So, first and foremost, write down your strengths and weaknesses in the following chart, after due deliberation. To cite an example, if you are adept at convincing people, then that is your strength; if not, it is a weakness. Your impressive speaking skills are your strength, but they are a weakness if the opposite is the case. Similarly, ascertain how you fare in other fields too, for instance, whether or not you are proficient in management. Having said that, nobody in this world is entirely perfect. Even if they are the greatest of saints, artists, scientists or businessmen...everybody inevitably possesses both strengths and weaknesses. Even so, the sole and significant difference is, great people are well aware of their positive and negative traits, while the common man is not. So, without further ado, compose a list of your five key strengths and weaknesses. Do not fall prey to any kind of misconception while making this list; make an inch-perfect one.

Your Strengths	Your Weaknesses
1	1 ....
....	....
....	....
....	....
....	....
....	....
....	....
....	....
....	....
....	....
....	....

2

2

3

3

4

4

5

5

Alright! Now that you have compiled this list, peruse it carefully, and comprehend all your strengths and weaknesses minutely and thoroughly. That is all! Kindly do not try to change your weaknesses, deeming them as your shortcomings. It doesn't matter if you are not good at speaking or if you lack convincing power, but if you try to rectify your weaknesses, you will veer off the path once again and fall prey to exploitation. Always bear in mind, despite having the gravest of weaknesses, many have scaled the ladder of success purely on the basis of a few strengths. Ergo, you must focus only on your strengths; instead of expending your energy in eradicating your weaknesses, focus on enhancing your strengths. For, to oust one's weaknesses is a gruelling quest, but it is fairly easy to enhance one's strengths. Hence, kindly focus on amplifying your strengths.

On this note, let me give you another practical piece of advice - as far as possible, engage only in the areas of your strength; do not try your hand in a field which exposes your vulnerability. If you lack proficiency in speaking a language, say, for instance, English, then avoid conversing in it before people; instead, it would serve you better to converse in your native tongue in which you are proficient. Similarly, if you lack effective conversational skills, then avoid indulging in excessive talking; instead, make it a habit to be brief and speak to the point. However, if you wish to practise speaking in English or improve your communication skills and become an effective speaker, then do so among your friends and family. But never try your hand in the fields in which you are out of your depth, in front of outsiders. For, a human being is an utterly fiendish creature; he never appreciates the strengths in a person, and instead, derives immense pleasure in scrupulously highlighting a person's weaknesses. This is the sole reason I am urging you to not dive into unfamiliar waters. Now, this is not at all difficult to remember, hence resolve and etch it in your mind to always leave a good impression. You will only showcase your strengths, and when the discussion veers close to your weaknesses, you will either remain quiet or cleverly evade the topic. You simply need to comprehend that progress and prosperity in life are attained when opportunities come your way, and opportunities are invariably provided by other people. Ergo, opportunities will knock on your door only if you hold sway over others. And if you wish to call the tune over others, then it is necessary to unfailingly showcase your strengths. And now that you have comprehended this point, I will share a valuable piece of advice with you. If you wish to gain influence over others, corner them in the field in which they are vulnerable. For example, if someone lacks proficiency in English and you start speaking to him in English, he will at least not be able to subjugate you. Furthermore, suitably impressed, he will not be able to pay attention to your weaknesses either. Moreover, due to his inability to speak fluently in English, he will fail to make an impression on you. In short, as far as possible, play to your strengths and the other person's weaknesses, and just watch how your influence over others inevitably soars. And then, this very influence will bring multiple opportunities in its wake.

The practical applications given above may seem trivial, but they hold the power to create wonders, simply because they are all psychologically sound. They are neither nonsensical nor fantastical notions that have the power to appeal, but inevitably fail when it comes to practical life. The applications I have listed here pertain to becoming your own doctor; it concerns gaining mastery over one's mind and life, even as one leads one's day-to-day life. So, I am confident that, one by one, you will put every application into practice in the manner suggested herewith, and in order to implement them scrupulously and suitably, draft a resolution for the same in your own words. Write in this resolution, "From this day onwards, I will engage only in the fields of my strengths; I will incessantly endeavour to play to my strengths. For, I have now realised that only my strengths can set me on the path of progress." Along with this, write down all the points which make this resolution unambiguous and effective to you, in your own words. This exercise will strengthen your resolve and fuel your determination with respect to your decision, because when you write the resolution in your own words, it will be ingrained in your mind forever.

Your Resolution

....

....

....

....

....

....

....

D) Define Who You Are

To begin with, answer a simple question - who are you? If truth be told, the majority of human beings are utterly confounded with regards to this question. If you ask someone to introduce themselves, for example, a doctor, they will state, 'I am a doctor, I belong to so and so caste, country and religion, and this is my clinic.' Am I right? Isn't this the manner in which one introduces oneself? Give it a thought, perhaps, you too must be furnishing a similar introduction of yourself, and presumably, you are not even aware that you can have any other introduction apart from this. Indeed, you must be commended for introducing yourself in this manner! What you are stating here as your introduction is as per other people's perspective. This is a practical introduction given in order to deal with worldly pursuits and engagements, so there is nothing wrong in giving this introduction to the world. But it is a matter of grave concern if, confused, you come to believe that, this is, indeed, who you are. Verily, the greater part of mankind is committing this grave mistake and is thus compelled to lead a superficial life. The truth is, only a handful of people in this world are living their lives in a state of total awareness. And verily, when you are not living keenly and deeply, how do you expect to achieve anything worthwhile in life? Is it any wonder then that a majority of human beings fail to do anything constructive? Whether it is in the sphere of professional or personal space, people are going about their activities on a superficial level, without putting their heart and soul in it. Pray tell me, if all your activities are performed on a superficial plane, listlessly and half-heartedly, how can you expect to lead a joyous life?

Ergo, if you wish to live your life to the fullest, draft your own definition of who you truly are, and reserve the definition that you have devised for the world only for the sake of worldly engagements. For, your present definition, vis-à-vis the world, defines your ego, not you; in fact, you are far more profound than your ego. Your current definition does not express who you are; it simply specifies your professional or educational qualifications, your religion, your worldly possessions and chattels, and so on. But who are you, really? The definition you have been carrying around for years is certainly not the answer to this question. For, you are not the ego, but the mind; you are not the *karta* i.e. doer, but the *karma* i.e. deed. Read that again, for the above-mentioned statement is extremely profound, and it is imperative for you to fathom its import. Grasp once and for all—your deeper existence is defined by the deed (*kriya*), not the doer *(karta)*. The doer, in this context, has a very superficial existence; and there is no fun in living a superficial life. Ergo, devise a new definition of your own with 'deed' at the centre of your personality. Leave your educational degrees, religion, community, house and car to the world and carve a new definition for yourself on the basis of your deeds. To materialise this, compile the list provided below with respect to your life after due deliberation, and incorporate your present tasks, relationships, hobbies, interests, etc. in this list.

Topic	List
Your current tasks	* Write down all the tasks you routinely undertake

Your present-day intimate relationships

* Note down the names of all the people with whom you are genuinely attached

Your hobbies

* Jot down all the pursuits which you are fond of and enjoy indulging in

Your other priorities

* List all the engagements which you can include neither in tasks nor hobbies

Your duties * Note down all the commitments, which you consider as mandatory to discharge

....

....

....

....

....

....

....

....

....

....

....

....

Now that I have provided you with a framework, compile the list with utmost care, on the basis of your present state of mind and life. It is imperative to consider your present state of mind and life, because your present is your very life, and even your future is determined by your present. So, without further ado, give your identity a new definition – the one you create on your own, in accordance with your mind, using this framework as your foundation. For example, if you are a doctor, you can write, "I am the act of performing surgery, which is verily my life and also my principal joy. Besides this, I am a mind engaged in lending pleasure to myself and my family, a mind which also delights in good food (and drink), playing chess and watching movies, whenever the opportunity presents itself. I am a mind engaged in safeguarding my health and happiness. I am a mind desirous of the progress of my family, a heart which beats with this desire day and night." Here, I have illustrated how you can forge your own definition, so write down an expansive definition of yourself, which encompasses all your deeds... And conceive the definition in the form of deeds, not doer.

My Definition

....

....

....

....

....

....

Now, you might well enquire, 'What will I gain by this new definition I have given to myself?' Well, did you not espy any benefit straightaway? Come on! You must have certainly perceived it, after all, you are not so ignorant! This seemingly brief definition, which I have bidden you to compose in the form of a deed, will leave an extremely profound impact on you and your life. First and foremost, this definition will help you discern yourself inside and out. Secondly, this definition will help you to effectively comprehend your present-day life. And the greatest benefit it will accrue is the immediate impairment of your ego. For, henceforth, you will confine your egoistic definition to worldly matters alone, and this will free your mind of all baggage and make it feel as light as a feather. By discarding this veneer of superficiality, you will feel as if a significant weight has been lifted off your shoulders, and you will consequently start living more and more naturally, with each passing day. Most importantly, having accepted yourself as a deed, you will undertake every task sincerely and wholeheartedly. And as a wonderful outcome of that, your life will change dramatically, and you will derive enjoyment from your work, family as well as your hobbies. That is because, you are now that deed itself. And when you lend your heart and mind wholly to everything you do, you will always abound with energy, and besides, you will be able to accomplish your tasks more efficiently and effectively. And this will, undoubtedly, make it easier for you to set yourself on the path of progress and prosperity.

Most significantly, consider this definition you have created for yourself as your 'Laxman Rekha'—the demarcation line that you must never step over. In other words, as far as possible, make sure you spend most of your time performing deeds in and around this definition, for when these deeds themselves define who you are, you will be able to accomplish them effortlessly. However, if you veer away from your definition and indulge in something else, apart from these deeds, you will find it cumbersome and invariably perform those deeds in a listless and apathetic manner. However, this is life; and you might be called upon to undertake some tasks that are not to your liking at all. So, in such a situation, if something crops up out of the blue, grin and bear it, and deal with it to the best of your ability; but strive to limit yourself to this definition as much as possible. In other words, try to stay true to your definition. By moulding yourself as per this practical application and living your life in sync with this definition, your life will begin to appear beautiful to you, and the belief that life is a burden, will weaken. You will no longer feel exhausted, and most importantly, you will gain clarity regarding your present state of mind and life.

E) Plan for Your Death

I am certain, now that you have been diligently employing the practical applications in your everyday life, you must have surely comprehended all your characteristics, traits and idiosyncrasies. You must have got a fair idea of who you are and what your strengths and weaknesses are. I am also confident that you must have settled down in your present life with unflinching fervour, resolutely and unwaveringly. Now, essay one final remedy – steer your life on the path of perfection. And in order to do so, you must swim against the tide; while everyone in this world makes plans for their life, you must plan for your death. That's right! And I will explain how to go about it. Furthermore, do not stop at planning; finalise the set of conditions, mental, physical and worldly, in which you wish to breathe your last. And determine all of this according to your nature; basically, you have to defer to your own self, even when making this decision. Similar to all previous cases, you have to become your own doctor and take the matter in your own hands in this case too.

Therefore, brace yourself to prepare for death. The only point to comprehend in this respect is, your happiness lies solely in that, which is in harmony with your nature. Your peace dwells where your mind bides. Thus, let your nature alone be the judge of the state in which you wish to bid adieu to this world. And at the outset, let me help you do so with the means of a chart. Firstly, you must recognise yourself truly and deeply and make up your mind concerning the following points vis-à-vis your last moments, and then, I will shed light on the next course of action.

Your options	Write at length what you wish for, in your own words
Do you wish to pursue work till the time you depart from this world or do you want to spend the last two decades of your life in retirement?	

Do you wish to be healthy and active or be ailing and in poor health when you pass away?

Note down the names of all the people with whom you wish to be on good terms till you breathe your last.

What are the things you want to know or comprehend before you bid adieu to this world?

What are the things you want to do before you die?

Determine the five things mentioned above, and once you have decided, set your present life in accordance with them. Remember, you were, are and will always remain the king of your life. You do not need to run helter-skelter seeking support in order to live your life well. Live your life as per your wishes and spend the last moments of your life exactly how you wish. Tap into the incredible strength of this great power of yours, and utilise it to your maximum benefit. In this verily lies your glory. As for the question of how to set your life by determining your last moment, I will elucidate it for you.

1. You want to spend the last two decades of your life as a retired person or a person of leisure

If you wish to spend the last two decades of your life in peaceful retirement, then you must commence doing two things diligently, right from today, or rather from this moment itself. First, execute your work with a staunch sense of commitment and sincerity, shielding yourself from idleness and laxity. Secondly, save systematically and consistently for the next twenty years. Remember, both this choice and this decision rest with you alone.

2. You wish to be hale and hearty till your last breath

If you wish to be in the pink of health until you bid adieu to the world, engage in some kind of physical activity for at least half an hour daily. Eat as per your constitution and do not skimp on sleep. However, the human body is an impish instrument; oft-times, it wreaks havoc even in the lives of those who do everything as per the book, while many a time, it spares the lives of those who act recklessly. Now, it is that *leela*, that play of life, over which nobody has any authority or control. However, with this step, you will at least set off in the right direction by exercising regularly and practising healthy sleep habits.

3. You wish to be on cordial terms with a particular set of people till your last breath

Again, it is you who has to decide on the people with whom you wish to maintain cordial relationships, until your last breath. And you have to make this decision hearkening to your heart. Of course, you will not wish your relations to sour with the people who are dear to you such as your spouse, parents, children, friends, and so on. Ergo, simply resolve to never engage in prolonged disagreements with the people you wish to be on good terms with till the end of your life's journey. Moreover, cultivate a habit of letting go of petty or trifling issues. Upon doing so, bitterness will never creep into your relationships with these people, and you will be able to maintain healthy and amicable relationships with them forever.

4. You wish to garner knowledge about certain subjects

Generally, we all desire to garner knowledge about certain subjects during our lifetime. So, why not cease squandering time over trivial matters, and instead, expend it in garnering knowledge about the topics we wish to explore and delve in. Each person wants to seek knowledge about a particular subject as per his interest; be it the DNA and genes, the moon and the stars, or spirituality and psychology. So, what are you waiting for? Immerse yourself into gaining knowledge about your field of interest, whenever you find the opportunity so that you do not have to spend the last moments of your life lamenting over unfulfilled wishes. The decision rests with you; if you do not wish the last moments of your life to be agonising, then allocate a portion of your day for this purpose, commencing from today itself.

5. You wish to engage in certain hobbies and activities

Every human being nurtures a fondness for a few hobbies and interests, whether it is engaging in sports, indulging in food, painting or playing the guitar. Ergo, whenever you get the chance to indulge in your hobbies, use it optimally. Life is short and you may not find the opportunities to indulge in your hobbies forever. Thus, it is better not to squander the last moments of your life bemoaning over all the activities and pleasurable pursuits you could not indulge in. A person of good sense that you are, I hope you will fathom the importance of this point; on my part, I have already given you a hint.

Now, let me reiterate the points I have mentioned thus far so that it is drilled into your psyche—understand clearly that you possess supreme authority over your life; Nature has accorded you the honour of being the undisputed king of your life. Why then do you not wish to live like a king and die a death befitting a king? This begets another question, what does it mean to live like a king? Well, the answer is quite simple - to do everything as per one's wishes, just like a king would. So, what is holding you back? Nothing, indeed! All you need to do is, fathom who you are and plan for your death day in such a way that you embrace death in a grand manner akin to a king. Verily, on your deathbed, at the time of crossing the great divide, you must be able to proudly declare that 'I did what I wanted to... I got what I wished for... and I lived my life the way I wanted to.' Plan to live the final moments of your life in this very state of ultimate contentment. Indeed, only a person who has spent his last moments in such a supreme state of contentment can be termed to have lived a successful life; all other pronouncements pertaining to success are superficial. I hope, after having imbibed these profound guidelines, you will plan for your death perfectly, and thereby, settle yourself on all fronts. The greatest benefit this will accrue is, you will no longer engage in myriad pointless pursuits that you are wont to otherwise, and at the same time, you will begin to live a focused life, following the dictates of your mind. Ideally, this is how one must live; discontentment of any kind should not haunt you at the time of death. So, without further ado, establish a solid foundation of the state you want to be in when you breathe your last, by becoming the doctor of every aspect of your life. For, the one whose death is set, his life is bound to be set. Ergo, resolve once and for all, when Nature has sent you in this world as a king, you will live like a king and die like one as well.

Pen Your Own Scripture to Progress in Life

Since aeons, humans have had recourse to a multitude of scriptures and a host of beliefs in order to prosper and progress in life. Revering them as sacred, the greater majority of people also recite them and meditate on them. So, why is everyone failing to set their lives on the path of progress? There is but one answer to this; life cannot prosper and progress by following the scriptures composed by other people, as the mindset of the composer of any scripture cannot help but prevail over his thoughts. That being the case, how can a contemporary human being, bearing an entirely different mindset and living in a completely different set of time, place and circumstances, be on the same wavelength as him? He certainly cannot be! But even so, blinded by ignorance, every person is bearing the burden of the scriptures penned by other people. Consequently, caught in this whirlpool, a majority of human beings find their lives burdensome. However, this does not imply the dearth of wise and learned men in history; the world has, indeed, played host to several wise beings, who have urged people to become their own doctor rather than trying to confuse them by devising (complicated and lengthy) scriptures. To illustrate this point, Krishna has not penned the *Vedas* nor has Christ composed the Bible...nor has Buddha written the *Buddha Shastra*. Buddha counsels one to become one's own light, while Krishna expounds, in this world, a person is himself his own friend and his own enemy. Even the great Chinese philosopher, Lao Tzu declares, the one who is wise is himself his own *guru*. But nobody wants to pay heed to the words of the wise, as they are all preoccupied in imbibing other people's opinions and beliefs.

Never mind! You are a sensible person, aren't you? Hence, you must not only become your own doctor, but also pen your own scripture; in other words, you must prepare your own list of dos and don'ts. Viewed from this perspective, not only are you reading this book but you are also composing your own scripture simultaneously, because all that you are writing in this book is verily your own scripture. I would like to reiterate; write everything in pencil. For, whatever you are writing is based on your present state of mind and life. However, following this scripture consistently, both your mind and life will gradually transform. And as you experience the transition and transformation, you will find that quite a few aspects of what you had written earlier no longer hold true. In that case, simply erase what you had written earlier and write afresh, because, after all, this book is your very own scripture.

You must refer to it repeatedly and also perpetually make changes in it in accordance with the changing time and circumstances. Besides, any scripture which is incapable of altering itself as per the changing times is of no use whatsoever! And that is precisely why most of the scriptures prove to be such dismal failures. Hence, I am asking you to write your scripture in pencil so that you can alter it in accordance with the changing times. I believe, by now, you must have realised the importance of composing your own scripture in order to set your life on the path of progress. And by virtue of penning your own scripture, you will also reclaim the reins of your life. In fact, this is the only choice you have! For, in this game of life, you are yourself the patient as well as the doctor. In this *leela*, this play of life, you are both the devotee as well as the God. So, gird up your loins and prepare yourself to play this game of life in the right manner, by liberating yourself from other people's scriptures, and instead, penning your own glorious one.

You are Ready to Take the First Concrete Step

You must have definitely put into practice all the practical applications provided so far, and by means of these applications, you must have certainly realised who you are inside and out. At the same time, you must have fathomed the intricacies of your mind, while most of your confusions regarding life must have also been banished. Consequently, your life must now be abounding with greater happiness, joy and peace than ever before. Furthermore, you might also be experiencing a surge in self-confidence and perseverance. But in case these changes have not come to pass, then know for sure that you have not properly implemented the practical applications provided so far. For, the core essence of what you are and what you should do next should have certainly become clear with the help of these applications. And I am certain that everything must have become crystal clear to most of the people reading this book. I am also sanguine that they must be leading happier and more confident lives now. And those who are still treading on shaky grounds, unsure of themselves, should not be in a rush to proceed ahead, but patiently read and grasp everything discussed till this point once again. For, at the outset, I had clarified that this is not a book, but your very own scripture. And just like a revered book, you have to hold on to it all your life and peruse it time and again. Thus, do not be hasty; pore over each aspect step by step, while proceeding slowly but steadily. Remember, all these deliberations and applications will directly affect your life, hence you must proceed with utmost patience. Comprehend well that even the smallest of premises given in this book is a kind of practical application, and viewed from this perspective, more than fifty practical applications are provided in this book. Thus, it is imperative to imbibe them patiently, in a step-by-step manner.

Having said that, I am sure everyone must have undertaken the journey till this point wisely and sagaciously. I am convinced that after successfully conducting your own surgery by becoming your own doctor, you are now ready and willing to engage in the race of life, primed with an indomitable spirit. Oh! You have absolutely no idea of how great a victory you have attained, by becoming your own doctor and performing your own surgery. Of course, your personality, having undergone a positive transformation, must have provided a glimpse of the giant strides you have made on this path thus far. So, what are you waiting for? Powered by this new and improved version of yours, start afresh and leap into life's journey, full of vim and vigour. Now, you are no longer confused; for, the path ahead is straight and crystal clear. Most importantly, you are also fortified by the blessings of Nature to embark on your new life, so continue to forge ahead with full confidence. Ah yes, one last point... I will apprise you of a few more practical applications as we proceed further in this book. Deliberate upon them, as you advance in your new life and endeavour to imbibe them as soon as possible. All of them are extremely simple; neither are they difficult to fathom nor cumbersome to put into practice. And once you have embraced them as well, you will be unstoppable. You will at once become unparalleled and perfect, ready to march ahead in the right direction in life. However, etch this deeply in your mind that I can only provide you with hints; ultimately, it is you who has to hold the scalpel and conduct your own surgery with absolute precision and perfection. I can assure you that post this successful surgery, not only your status and prestige, but your sway will scale its zenith too. My humble request to you is, immerse yourself in this book with concentration, thoughtfulness and a calm and serene mind, and imbibe every word of wisdom slowly and patiently; as for the rest, your transformed personality will take care of it automatically. With this, I hope you are completely ready to commence the next stage of your surgery!

Determine Your Dos and Don'ts Yourself

All teachings and counsel, whether offered by society, religion, family or intelligent folks comprise just one component – dos and don'ts. All teachings boil down to which actions one must perform and which one must refrain from. Furthermore, the number of lists of dos and don'ts circulating around us are not confined to a minuscule few. If you put together all the dos and don'ts in the world, this number will easily scale millions! In such a case, it is well-nigh impossible to imbibe the knowledge of all prescribed dos and don'ts; perhaps, one needs fifty births simply to glean the content of such humungous lists! Besides, all such lists of dos and don'ts defy each other; what falls in the category of dos in list A is included in the category of don'ts in list B. In fact, these lists are so ambiguous and contradictory in nature that it is difficult to gauge which list is right and which is wrong.

So, what is one supposed to do then? Well, nothing much; all you need to do is, become your own *guru*. Turn a deaf ear to the dos and don'ts devised by other people, for they are entirely superfluous and irrelevant. Life is just another name for constantly changing circumstances, hence, eventually, it is a person's own good sense that serves him best. So, from now onwards, adopt only two kinds of teachings, one which enhances your comprehension power, and the other, which teaches you how to become your own *guru*. If you wish to set your life on the path of progress, then, at the very least, put a stop to blindly adopting the lists of dos and don'ts prescribed by others.

Tell yourself, 'When both I and the composers of these endless lists of dos and don'ts belong to the same ilk of human race, why should I live my life abiding by others' teachings? When it is but my life we are speaking of, then its dos and don'ts will also be devised by me. I will turn a deaf ear to any other set of dos and don'ts, regardless of the book that they are mentioned in or the prodigy of the person making the said pronouncements.' Nevertheless, bear in mind, this does not imply defying or violating traffic rules or other rules laid down by legal authorities for the purpose of law and order; those rules can't be neglected and we simply must abide by them, for, they are laid down for our own convenience. Here, we are referring to the rules devised for your personal life, where nobody, except for yourself, must have the right to make decisions for you. In fact, it is in your best interest to make all those decisions yourself.

Having said that, I am fully aware that it is no cakewalk to put this into practice. But this is the sole recourse you have if you wish to have a firm, unwavering personality and become attuned with Nature. Besides, do you not find the notion of other people pronouncing the decisions of your life a bit strange? Does it not bother you that others decide what food you may eat and which edifices you may enter? You are a human being and you know full well what is good for you. For that matter, nobody is better aware of this than you, because this is verily Nature's design for humankind. Even so, you doggedly adhere to these lists of dos and don'ts, imposed upon you by others, failing to grasp that they invariably debilitate your personality. Ergo, compose your own dos and don'ts, for, nobody can think of your best interests better than you. This is the least you can do for your own sake, and I am sure that you will certainly do it. Oh! You cannot even fathom how liberated you will feel once you have broken free from the shackles of other people's dos and don'ts! As the burden imposed by others lifts off from your shoulders, you will feel as light as a feather; trust me, it will be a novel and incredible experience altogether. Once you break free of these inane and nonsensical chains of slavery, your personality will blossom like a flower and become far more impressive than before. And in order to ease this process for you, I will assist you with a chart. You simply have to fill up the chart provided below after due deliberation; begin by jotting down five key dos and don'ts, which have been thrust upon you. Once you relinquish these, you will find the task of letting go of the rest absurdly easy. For, once somebody acquires a taste for freedom, he automatically applies himself to breaking free from all kinds of bondages. So, fill the chart provided below with utmost care, giving it due consideration. Do not make haste and fill in the blank spaces unthinkingly; fill it calmly, taking your time to ponder over each point. I'm placing quite a bit of emphasis on this, because the slavery of the human mind dates back to centuries, and by now, it has probably assumed the form of fear. But if you make a start and persevere nonetheless, you will doubtless get delivered from this thraldom as well. So now, without further ado, concentrate on the chart below and begin the process.

Write, at length, about the dos and don'ts thrust upon you by others, which you abide by	
Dos thrust by others	**Don'ts thrust by others**
1	1 ....
....	....
....	....
....	....
....	....
....	....
....	....
....	....
....	....
....	....

2

2

3

3

4

4

5

5

Reflect on all your answers and astutely resolve that from this very moment, you will steer clear of all the dos and don'ts thrust upon you by others. Once you have relinquished these impositions, put a tick mark accordingly in the box provided below.

1 Do you not feel as if these dos and don'ts pose a threat to your freedom?

☐ Yes ☐ No ☐ Relinquished these impositions

2 Do you always follow them absolutely and unconditionally?

☐ Yes ☐ No ☐ Relinquished these impositions

3 Does the thought of giving them up scare you?

☐ Yes ☐ No ☐ Relinquished these impositions

4 Are these being followed by the entire world?

☐ Yes ☐ No ☐ Relinquished these impositions

5 Has ruin befallen those who are not abiding by them?

☐ Yes ☐ No ☐ Relinquished these impositions

After penning down the five key dos and don'ts, which others have forced upon you, and having subjected them to close scrutiny in the second chart, you must have noticed that they all jeopardise your ultimate freedom. Furthermore, you must have realised that all these dos and don'ts are nothing save for an indication of your fear, and they give rise to vague and strange fears for no reason at all. Besides, you must have also woken up to the fact that these dos and don'ts are not being followed by the world at large; in fact, the ones not abiding by them are thriving and flourishing nonetheless. In other words, no harm befalls a person who is not abiding by them. Why then must one subject oneself to slavery and nurse all kinds of fears? Thus, resolve once and for all that 'I free myself from the dos and don'ts thrust upon me by others.' For, why adhere to rules that snatch away the ultimate freedom bestowed by Nature? Besides, if you manage to escape their suffocating grip in some instances, why not shake them off for good? So, do whatever it takes to wake up to this truth and banish these dos and don'ts from your life forever. And as soon as you have freed yourself of them, put a tick mark in the last box provided in the chart above. The psychological significance of getting liberated from the dos and don'ts thrust upon you by others is great indeed. For, not only will it set you free but it will also sharpen your decision-making skills. Furthermore, no sooner you unshackle yourself from their stifling bonds than your personality will also shine. Thus, persevere and get through this little struggle by yourself and emerge triumphant. For, once you prevail in this struggle, you will soon triumph over all of life's struggles.

I hope, you will resolve to steer clear of these futile bondages, and additionally, pen down a determined resolution in your own words to this effect. Each word that you pen yourself has the power to wield a tremendous influence, because the writing that flows from your own pen commits you to the very cause; in fact, writing by yourself is akin to making a vow to yourself. I well know its significance, therefore, I extend my best wishes to you in advance. I hope, hereafter, you will certainly liberate yourself from the dos and don'ts imposed upon you by others. Freeing yourself from their clutches is vital, for, unbeknownst to you, it is these very dos and don'ts that underlie most of your fears and apprehensions. And as long as you are inexorably held captive in their clutches, you will invariably be scared and anxious for one reason or another. And pray tell me, what is a fearful person good for? Why, nothing at all, because neither is he able to enjoy his life nor is he able to accomplish anything great in life. Hence, it is imperative for you to pass this test; remember, freedom and fearlessness are essential if you wish to make a difference and leave your mark on this world. If you are a lion, then proudly dwell in the wilderness; why languish in the circus like a puppet, doing everyone's bidding? With this, I have galvanised you as much as I possibly could; now the decision rests with you to break free from this servile mindset you have shrouded yourself in. And I am certain, you will at least do this much to set your life on the path of progress. So, come, pen a firm resolution for it in your own words and meditate upon these resolutions till the time you do not break free from the clutches of these enslavements.

Resolution in your own words

....

....

....

....

....

....

....

....

Furthermore, you must comprehend that every era, situation, person and life is radically different. So, how can anybody else's dos and don'ts be the least bit useful to you? Besides, just think, what does it mean to be a human being? It bespeaks a person who is sensible.

And when a human being is so sensible, he is obviously fully cognisant of his life, and is able to discern what is good and bad for him, while also being keenly aware of his virtues and vices. It is only on account of the shackles of slavery he has embraced that he fails to follow through on his own words determinedly. And almost every human being finds himself in this same sinking boat. To illustrate the above point, despite knowing that pursuing something will be beneficial for you, you find yourself incapable of executing it. Similarly, despite knowing that a bad habit is ruining your life, you are unable to forsake it. In other words, you fail to safeguard your interests, in spite of fervently wishing to do so. Do you know why you hold back in such situations? The answer is simple...because you have acquired a slavish mindset on account of abiding by other people's dos and don'ts; a mindset which can demonstrate circus tricks at the crack of a whip, but which is (oddly enough) not listening to the sound of its own doom! That is why, I am urging you to free yourself from the dos and don'ts forced upon you by others, for this will result in you reclaiming the reins of your life in your own able hands once again. Besides, you are fully cognisant of what is good and bad for you, and you also know your life inside and out. Thus, having freed yourself from the lists of dos and don'ts prescribed by others, ascertain three principal dos and don'ts for yourself, which best serve your interests and write them in your own words in the space given below. Then, every day, sit in solitude and ponder over them, till the time you begin to abide by them. Motivate yourself and commit yourself to diligently abide by them each day. Moreover, reneging on the dos and don'ts that you have composed yourself will not be so easy, because when you are tempted to flout them, your own written words will come to your mind. So, slowly but surely, through constant deliberation, you will inevitably succeed in this endeavour. What are you waiting for then? Grab a pencil and with full awareness, frame three key dos and don'ts that you wish to abide by. And just watch, how your life gets transformed right before your eyes, simply abiding by them! That is why, I urge you to become your own doctor, for there is no greater surgeon who can treat you better than you yourself.

Dos which I shall embrace from today onwards

1

2

3

Don’ts which I shall desist from today onwards

1

2

3

You may be wondering, why am I attaching so much importance to breaking free from the dos and don'ts prescribed by others and urging you to compose your own set of dos and don'ts? Well, let me elucidate its significance through the example of Bhagavad Gita, the oldest and most widely read text of theistic science in the world. The Bhagavad Gita commences with Arjuna's outright refusal to fight the war. And the excuses that Arjuna furnishes for his refusal are verily the dos and don'ts recorded in the *Vedas* and the scriptures. He solemnly apprises Krishna, 'Such conduct is not seemly as per the *Vedas* and the scriptures. It is not righteous to slay our brothers, relatives and teachers, for, such acts, in the scriptures, are termed as grave sins.' However, Krishna expresses his disagreement with Arjuna's declaration and asserts that the dos and don'ts prescribed by others are of no relevance to us. How can anybody heed them, when they are worth naught?! Further, Krishna goes on to state, 'Every human being has his own distinct dos and don'ts. O Arjuna, you are well aware of the whys and wherefores of this war, and here, you stand on the battlefield on account of those very reasons. So, it is you who must decide whether or not to fight this war, in view of your mind and life. Pray tell me, how are the dos and don'ts stipulated by religion and scriptures related with this?' Furthermore, Krishna pronounces that the person who abides by the dos and don'ts of others, forever finds himself swirling in a vortex of fear and confusion. And throughout the course of the Gita, as we have seen, Arjuna was not only confused but terrified as well. That is precisely why, Krishna explains to Arjuna that fear is engendered by following the religion prescribed by other people, and both fear and confusion can be dispelled only by following one's own religion. Following one's own religion implies living by the dos and don'ts which one has forged oneself. Bear in mind, here, Krishna is not speaking of being a follower of any religion such as Hinduism, Islam, Christianity, etc. Why, Krishna has not uttered the word 'Hindu' even once throughout his enunciation of the Gita! Krishna is speaking of matters that are eternal, which far transcend religion, caste and country, and that is why, the Bhagavad Gita is a 'universal masterpiece' which belongs to one and all. I believe, you must have now comprehended the significance of freeing yourself from the dos and don'ts of others, and must also be apprehending the merits of composing one's own dos and don'ts.

Therefore, simply continue drafting your own list of dos and don'ts in view of your life, using your own life's experiences as its foundation. It is perfectly fine to derive inspiration from others while compiling this list, but eventually, they must be your own specific dos and don'ts. Moreover, since this is not a religious or social obligation, you don't need to be rigid while following them. Your dos and don'ts are unlike the Bible or any other religious book for that matter, where there is no leeway to alter a single word, in spite of being proven erroneous. Nor are they so hidebound that one will simply have to tote the rules of the days of yore, despite living in the space age. These are one's personal dos and don'ts, drafted for one's own edification, so whenever there is a change in your mindset and your life, tweak your dos and don'ts accordingly. It is only for this reason that I am asking you to write everything in pencil, so that you can erase what you had written earlier and write afresh, as you march along with the changing times. And only those pronouncements, which we can write and erase ourselves, are efficacious and those alone can be termed our scripture. A true scripture is one which can be drafted, followed and altered according to the changing times, by our own selves, without succumbing to any kind of fear or confusion. Ergo, fill in your three principal dos and don'ts in the space provided in this book, and then every week, take time out to deliberate over them. When your life or priorities undergo a change, promptly erase the old ones and replace them with the new, altered ones. Persistently evaluate your list on a weekly basis, for, you are, after all, the author of this scripture. And then, live your life in accordance to the scripture penned by you; trust me, no fear or confusion will ever plague you. And then, just behold the remarkable transformation your life will undergo with this one constructive step. So, without further ado, make a firm resolution and abide by it. As an initial step, begin with this process, and as we proceed further, I will help you frame some other dos and don'ts which are even more vital. I will guide you in drafting a permanent list of your dos and don'ts, which will serve as an invaluable guide in every situation and circumstance in your life. These will be dos and don'ts which need not be erased and written anew; or in other words, the eternal dos and don'ts which you cannot claim have been forced upon you by someone else. These dos and don'ts will be ready reckoners, standing unflinchingly by your side, always there to jump to your aid. I would, thus, like to suggest a few plain and simple dos and don'ts, which will transform you into an exceptional personality, as soon as you include them in your list. I am sanguine that you are all well and truly prepared for this life-changing experience. However, at this juncture, let me reiterate, if other people's dos and don'ts still hold sway over you, then you will never be able to staunchly abide by these eternal dos and don'ts. However, I am positive that after this in-depth discussion, you would have definitely made a resolute decision to follow the dos and don'ts composed by your own self.

1. Serving your own self is verily your religion and foremost duty

Life is an opportunity and you are fortunate enough to have attained this wonderful opportunity to live. And when you have been granted this opportunity, it behoves you to make the most of it and live your life to the fullest. Having said that, what does it really mean to live to the fullest? Indubitably, if your mind abounds with joy, merriment, peace and other positive emotions, then it can be said that you are alive and have lived your life to the hilt. But if you continually find yourself in the clutches of worry and frustration, then that is called leading an insentient existence, which is as good as living like a corpse. By and large, everyone is cognisant of this fact, and that is why, everyone wishes to live their lives happily and peacefully. However, this begs the question, what is holding them back from living a happy life? When posed with this question, most people bemoan that others have made their life hellish, making it impossible for them to live happily. And therein lies the answer...because one places the blame on others, one finds himself unable to live to the fullest. Comprehend clearly that a joyous and carefree life will elude you till the time you do not break the habit of blaming others for your miserable state. Besides, have a think, who is charged with the responsibility of ushering laughter, happiness and merriment in your life? Is it God, society, family, relatives, saints or social workers? Take your time and reflect on this question. Are you ready to answer? If yes, then tell me, with whom lies the onus of lending you happiness and peace? Got yourself in a tangle, haven't you? My friend, haven't you grasped yet that none of those mentioned above are responsible for setting your life on the path of progress; this is solely your responsibility and it is best for you to shoulder it yourself. Hence, stop squandering your energy in vain pursuits, and instead, make serving yourself your sole religion. All other religions that you know of may or may not prove useful to you, but this religion will indubitably prove of great worth to you. Ergo, from this day onwards, start serving yourself as much as possible. Accord the highest priority to your peace, merriment, happiness, work, sleep and health. Guard them all fiercely and make no mistake of considering this as selfishness, for this is verily your duty unto your own self; whereas selfishness is furthering one's own interest by inflicting harm or detriment upon others. Lies, theft and deceitfulness are all warning signs of selfishness. You certainly do not have to stoop low and demean yourself by resorting to any of these means; all you have to do is safeguard your mind, body and life. I would request everyone to serve themselves as best as they can, because if everybody were to live in the manner I have suggested, then nobody in the world will ever be dispirited or miserable. Thus, everybody must first effect their own betterment to the best of their ability. Whether it was Buddha or Christ, they too took care of their own well-being first and only then turned their attention towards working for the betterment of the world. For, effecting the betterment of the world is always secondary in importance. Speaking in logical terms, how can a person who is himself miserable, dispel the sorrows of the world? You verily cannot pour from an empty cup! Despite having good intentions, such a person will only spread misery and sorrow, and this is exactly the present state of the world. In today's world, the majority of people who are themselves unhappy, have turned into religious *gurus* and social workers. So, kindly put an end to this farce. Before attempting to draw grandiose schemes to resolve the problems of others, first serve your own self to the fullest. When your own sorrows and anguish are eliminated, you can endeavour to alleviate the grief and woes of others. But until then, please refrain from such endeavours, else you will only invite trouble. And since everybody is committing this self-same mistake, the world is overrun with despondent people.

Having understood that, comprehend clearly what is meant by serving your own self. Serving yourself implies taking utmost care of your own self and making optimum use of all the opportunities that grant you laughter, happiness and merriment. Prioritise your rest, recreation and health, and as far as possible, avoid engaging in acts which cause you hardship. Do not let others stand as an obstacle in the path of your happiness and well-being, and in case others act as an impediment, ignore them. But regardless of the prevailing circumstances, pave the way for happiness and energy to surge into your life. At the same time, in order to live a prosperous life, perform your tasks with utmost sincerity and diligence, for if your tasks leave much to be desired, and you are not sincere while performing them, your life will invariably be ruined. Thus, you will have to be mindful of this for the sake of safeguarding your own self. This will eventually augment your happiness and empower you to do good unto others to the best of your ability. For that matter, perceived from a psychological standpoint, only if you are happy and joyous yourself, can you really effect other people's betterment. But here, you must also comprehend that being mindful of your happiness does not mean troubling others. You must in no way force or browbeat others; in fact, you do not have any right to do so. You simply have to focus on your own happiness, without dependence on anyone. Neither must you harass others nor let others become an impediment in this course. Why don't you realise that your vexed and despondent state speaks volumes of you not having served yourself well. So, take good care of yourself and pamper yourself to the hilt. I reiterate that life is a splendid opportunity, and in order to make the most of this opportunity, you alone have to take care of yourself.

By the same token, if you wish to make your life beautiful, you must start composing your own *mantras*. On this note, comprehend another significant law of life; the only *mantras* that will serve you well in this world are the ones which you have composed yourself, for only such *mantras* can lend you firmness and constancy. Besides, do not make feeble pronouncements such as 'I take an oath' or 'I swear to God' when drafting your *mantras*. There is just one thumb rule to follow when composing one's own *mantras*...a firm resolve. In other words, you do not have to take oaths or make lofty proclamations; rather you have to resolve to serve yourself to the best of your ability, from the present moment itself. And in order to do so, write the *mantra* in your own words, because a *mantra* written in one's own words holds immense power. And constant contemplation over it in solitude enhances your perseverance and resolution manifold. Come, as this is the first *mantra* of your life, I will provide you a little assistance.

Mantra

I hereby resolve that from this day onwards, I will accord the highest priority to serving myself. I resolve that from this point onwards, I will not unduly trouble myself; instead, I will marshal all my resources to take good care of my health and happiness. And neither will I bother anybody nor let anybody become an impediment in this course. I staunchly resolve that from this moment onwards, I will take utmost care of myself; I will not live a lacklustre life nor will I die listlessly. Come hell or high water, I will find a way to live my life to the fullest, even in the toughest of circumstances...

With this, I have assisted you in composing your first *mantra*. Now, the onus shifts onto you; write it in your own words and ponder over it in solitude whenever you get an opportunity to do so. This will suffuse you with the determination to safeguard yourself and your life, and with this single change, your life will brim over with an abundance of happiness and joy. Consequently, you will abound with energy and vitality, and henceforth, you will also be able to perform your tasks more efficiently and effectively. So, without further ado, write down your *mantra* in your own words.

Your *Mantra*

....

....

....

....

....

....

....

....

2. Always ensure that whatever you say carries weight

Always bear in mind that more often than not, opportunities to progress in life, make way into our lives through others. For this reason, it is imperative that every word uttered by you carries weight, because the day people begin to perceive you as an idle chatterer, you forfeit the priceless opportunity to attain progress in life. Nobody will then pay heed to your words, and in that case, the likelihood of a great opportunity coming your way through someone else will also dwindle to naught. That is why, I state that it is vital for everything you speak to have merit. This, however, does not necessitate you to share your suggestions or opinions on every single matter. In fact, it is far better to speak pithily than ramble endlessly without substance. So, henceforth, make a firm resolve to only speak on subjects you are well-informed about and refrain from jumping into conversations with half-baked knowledge. Observing restraint in speech is definitely acceptable than talking through your hat and being proved wrong time and again. Once people look down upon you as a silly flibbertigibbet, your very identity stands the risk of being devalued. So, play the joker, crack jokes, chitter-chatter and talk about everything under the sun without thinking twice, but when you have to opine on subjects of import, speak only when you are well-versed in the particular topic. Else, simply focus on listening to and comprehending what others have to say; this will help enhance your personality and make a positive impact on people. Remember, lack of knowledge regarding a subject is not a crime. You lose nothing in keeping quiet and listening to others speak; but it is, indeed, a folly, when the words uttered by you prove to be wrong. Thus, I sincerely hope, you will bring about this positive change in your personality. Ergo, promptly write a resolution in your own words for the same, as you are no longer a novice in drafting resolutions. And consider the resolution written by you as a *mantra* for yourself.

Your *Mantra*

....

....

....

....

....

....

....

....

3. Set your routine

Before we begin this topic, answer a question - what according to you is the game of life all about? Can a human being set his routine as per his whims and fancies? Obviously not! That being the case, grasp once and for all that the game of life is already set by Nature and no human being can build his own specific routine, isolated from the design of Nature. And as per the routine set by Nature, every person in this world must work for approximately eight hours every day in order to lead an honourable life. Even if one is a homemaker, one still has to spend about eight hours every day in household work. Likewise, every person needs around eight hours of sleep each day, while in the remaining eight hours, everybody has to manage their routine tasks. Additionally, in this same set of eight hours, a person has to squeeze in time for recreation and pleasure. This is verily Nature's design for a human being and the latter has been bound in this routine since the inception of human civilisation. Furthermore, this eight-hour triad is fully interconnected and interdependent; to illustrate, a disruption in your sleep will invariably impact your work. If you are unable to give your best to your work, you will find yourself incapable of enjoying yourself or sleeping soundly at night. Likewise, if one is bereft of time to rest and enjoy, it becomes difficult for one to concentrate on work. In other words, it is vital for every segment of life to be spent in a satisfactory manner, and only if one sails through in this seamless manner, can one truly state that one is living a blissful and well-settled life. As you know full well, your life is wrecked when you fail to be productive, because in such a case, you might find yourself in dire straits financially. On the other hand, at the physical level, you feel listless and everything seems dull and lacklustre when you do not get enough sleep, for the mind is wearied, deprived of adequate rest and recreation. In such a case, you simply do not have the energy to undertake tasks. Basically, the majority of people are falling short in one segment or the other; some are troubled on account of their inability to sleep adequately, while others become restless due to their inability to carve out time for leisure pursuits. Similarly, it is a common grievance of the greater majority of people that they find themselves unable to concentrate on their work.

However, from this day forth, put your life on track and resolve that you will sleep well, enjoy yourself and also perform your work sincerely and wholeheartedly. Although, this is easier said than done, for, man's nature is such that the moment he tries to grab hold of one part, the other part slips away from his grasp. Never mind! If you are unable to balance the three segments of your life on a daily basis, try to balance them on a weekly basis. Reserve the weekends for adjustment. If there is a deficit in your sleep during the week, catch up on your sleep over the weekend. If you are weary, having overworked through the week and your mind craves enjoyment, then gratify it with leisure and pleasure on the weekend. And if you have not been able to complete your work adequately during the course of the week and you have leeway to work over the weekends, then finish your work over the weekend. In other words, settle the week's account in that particular week itself. Resolve that at the end of the week, all three elements, sleep, work and recreation, should be fulfilled, as per necessity. This will enhance your performance in every sphere and open the doors to your progress; and needless to say, your life will always abound with merriment and zest. Note that nothing is coming undone, but if you fail to achieve an appropriate balance of work, sleep and recreation, a multitude of problems will start thronging your life. Thus, week by week, (do not fail to) fulfil these needs as per necessity, for, if you leave a great deal to be desired, it will beget endless trouble. You will lose out on the many joys of life, and besides, you will be left empty-handed in the end. I am sanguine, you must have comprehended the gist, and from now onwards, you will reserve the weekend to balance the elements that were left unfulfilled during the week. On the weekend, you will take care of whichever segment you had slipped up in during the week. But yes, if the nature of your work is such that you cannot adjust it over the weekend, then undertake your work so sincerely and diligently during the week that you only have to make adjustments for your sleep and recreation over the weekend. In order to do justice to life, one has to find ways and means to that effect; that is to say, each person has to strike a proper balance of work, sleep and leisure within the framework of his life. And it is imperative for every person to strike this balance, for, once you are able to find the perfect balance, everything else will also seamlessly fall into place. Then, not only will you be able to undertake your work effectively and efficiently, but you will also be able to lend the much-needed amusement and recreation to your mind. And when these two aspects are taken care of, you will invariably sleep like a baby!

In other words, achieving a fine balance in the three segments of life is a prerequisite to living a complete and fulfilled life. This is, in sooth, Nature's design for a human being, and this is precisely why, all three dimensions of life, namely sleep, work and recreation, are completely interdependent. If one of these segments slips out of balance, it straightaway impacts the other two. And if this balance continues to be disrupted on a regular basis, then life's wagon slides off the track, and all that one is left with is utter exhaustion and fatigue. And I certainly do not wish anybody to get trapped in this labyrinth, nor do I want your life to become a millstone around your neck. This is the reason why, I have provided you with the only solution that can help you safeguard yourself from this plight—find the perfect balance in all three segments of life—and never mind even if that balance is achieved on a weekly basis.

I'm sure you must have apprehended the import of my words, so cast aside all other tasks and accord first priority to balancing these three segments of your life on a weekly basis. There should neither be mental exhaustion nor physical fatigue in life; mental tiredness will be dispelled by amusement and diversion, while physical exhaustion will be obliterated by sleep and exercise. And if these two are perfectly balanced, the quality of your work will improve manifold, thereby guaranteeing your progress. So, write down your *mantra* in your own words that 'not only will I ensure that my sleep, work and recreation are effectively balanced on a weekly basis, but I will also accord the highest priority to striking the right balance between these three aspects.' Write this down in your own words, and then, every Saturday morning, deliberate over this *mantra*. Take stock of the aspect that is falling short at the end of the week and then make sure you replenish it. Here, you must also bear in mind that different people have different sleep requirements, so everybody must sleep as per their body's dictates. Likewise, each person finds amusement in different pursuits, so each person must indulge in that which gives him pleasure, for, all that matters is to pamper, amuse, delight and rejuvenate the mind. Ergo, draft this resolution in your own words and consider it as a *mantra* conceived for your own self, and then, proceed accordingly, composing your life's scripture.

Your *Mantra*

....

....

....

....

....

....

....

....

4. Learn to gauge the math of time and energy.

You must certainly be proficient in mathematical calculations in practical life, for this skill is vital in order to survive in the world. However, your mathematical wizardry must extend to the profundity of life too. In a human being's lifespan, the time at his disposal is limited to 80–100 years. Viewed from this perspective, no commodity in life is more valuable than time, but due to your naivety, you never maintain any record of time. You fritter away days, months and years in pointless deeds, and eventually, you find yourself in such a deplorable state that you fall short of time to undertake important tasks. Likewise, you abuse your energy as well. Nobody in this world has unlimited reserves of energy, but even so, you continue with your foolish ways, squandering your energy in endless futile pursuits. The primary reason behind this is, the greater majority of people are ignorant about the ultimate law of life, which is—there are no free lunches in this world and you have to invariably pay the price for everything. Viewed from this perspective, life is akin to a business transaction, and only a person who buys for less and sells for more earns a profit. Although you follow this theory in conventional worldly trade, you slip up in the most crucial dealings of life. You simply fail to realise that in order to attain success and prosperity, you require both time and energy, and both the resources are limited in quantity. Impervious to the significance of time and energy, you continue to expend them in a foolhardy manner. As a consequence, you are eventually stripped of the time and energy required to undertake the prime tasks of life, and this, in fact, is the main reason for all of life's failures. I hope you must have adequately grasped this theory expounded here in brief.

Thus, apprehend the significance of time and energy from now on, and learn to calculate and invest them dexterously. Comprehend once and for all that it is a give-and-take world, and you cannot gain anything in exchange for nothing; besides, not every precious commodity comes with a price tag. Barring monetary transactions, you have to pay the price for the majority of things using the currency of time and energy, so do not presume that the things you receive without paying money are coming to your lot for free. You are unquestionably paying their price in terms of your invaluable time and energy. Ergo, from this day forth, calculate minutely the time and energy required, prior to undertaking any task. If what you procure in return is more rewarding than the time and energy you expend while performing the said task, then go ahead and perform the task; but if the contrary is true, then refrain from it. The sky will not come crashing down upon you if you do not engage in a particular task. Once you become proficient in this crucial calculation, miracles will begin to manifest in your life. You will refrain from engaging in numerous pointless and unrewarding tasks that you are wont to do, leaving you with ample time and energy to undertake the tasks that truly matter. At present, you are at a stage where you make haste and foolishly scramble to undertake pointless pursuits, without carefully considering the logistics of the time and energy required for the task; this foolhardiness eventually leaves you with no time to perform the vital tasks. Thereafter, sapped of energy, you are unable to engage in your favourite tasks and pursuits. That is why, more often than not, you are unable to perform to your optimum best when it is most required. Believe me when I say that this is not the experience of just a few people but a sizeable majority! Why do you not comprehend, your life will prosper and progress only by way of performance, and both time and energy are absolutely essential to perform at your best.

I have explained to the best of my ability; the ball is in your court now, and it is you who has to put these learnings into practice. Therefore, never get mired in vain pursuits to the extent that you no longer have time for yourself or for undertaking important tasks. Likewise, do not tire yourself out by performing pointless tasks so much that you find yourself drained of energy and unable to perform when it is required the most. If no meaningful task calls for your attention, then sit down in calm and peace, enjoying your own company. You simply don't realise that your energy is depleted even by sitting glued to the TV for hours or by talking incessantly on the phone. All these pursuits also make you weary when you indulge in them beyond a limit. Ergo, if you wish to prosper and progress, you must learn to enjoy the solitude of your own being. Do not seek frivolous and futile tasks on account of idle restiveness. Verily, if you wish to safeguard your life, shield yourself from unnecessary activities and tiredness. For, you can attain progress and prosperity only by indulging in the required amount of leisure; that alone will help revitalise you and add vigour to your actions; and only if you have time on hand and are full of verve and energy, will you be able to utilise opportunities in an optimal manner. In this regard, let me also warn you, if exhaustion grips you beyond a point, then it will start reflecting on your face; all of a sudden, you will look worn out, far older than your age. Therefore, safeguard yourself from fatigue as much as possible. Do not expend all your life energy on vain pursuits; else, you will lose the zest for life eventually. As a consequence, you will exhaust your ability to forge ahead, and the day will not be far when life will seem akin to a losing battle. And once you slip into this dangerous abyss, you will never be able to change your life (for the better) again.

Thus, draft a resolution for conserving time and energy in your own words. Resolve that not only will you spend leisure time with yourself, but you will also abound with energy. And in order to do so, you will avoid engaging in pointless pursuits so that you can give a brilliant performance at the required moment. Simply write this down in your own words and keep reiterating this *mantra* in your mind. Believe me, the day you stop expending your time and energy unnecessarily, your life will automatically start scaling newer heights. Ergo, write down a *mantra* for yourself in your own words.

Your *Mantra*

....

....

....

....

....

....

....

....

5. Indulging in hobbies is pivotal to life

Energy is vital, both to enjoy life as well as to attain progress and prosperity. But wherefrom does one acquire this precious energy? For, in today's age of rush and haste, everybody is undoubtedly experiencing a paucity of energy; weariness and fatigue have plagued one and all. In such a bleak scenario, it is imperative for one to know what the principal source of energy is. So, let me acquaint you with the two key reservoirs of energy. First is the time spent in solitude, serenity and tranquillity. Unfortunately, in today's world, this is deemed as a pointless waste of time. The majority of people are simply incapable of sitting in solitude, thus, losing out on the great opportunity of tapping into the vast reservoir of mental energy. Therefore, spend a little time with yourself each day. You have absolutely no idea of the extent to which you will abound with energy with this single exercise, for, it will lend you freshness and alleviate the restlessness of your mind. Most of the great people in the world invariably spend hours in their own company, without engaging in any activity. Therefore, you too must start spending some time in peace by yourself; ensure that you spend at least ten minutes with yourself each day, post waking up and ten minutes before drifting off to sleep in the night. Likewise, indulging in hobbies with unrestrained enthusiasm and zeal is the second vital source of energy. Surely, each one of us enjoys some hobby or the other, be it travelling, sports, reading, savouring varied cuisines, and so on. Besides, life is a one-time opportunity and you have the chance to indulge in your hobbies only until you are alive. So, never suppress your interests; do not let them perish away in the grind of constraints and compulsions of life. Indulge in your hobbies unreservedly, whenever you get the chance, with the aid of whatever means is available at your disposal. Remember, hobbies have nothing to do with good-bad or virtue-sin. It is the dull, drab and lifeless people leading a listless life themselves, who have labelled habits, interests and passions as bad, by drafting lists of good-bad and virtue-sin. Ergo, consider every interest or hobby of yours as your *dharma*, your duty; for indulging in your hobbies will turn you into a powerhouse of energy. However, it is imperative to comprehend the correct definition of hobby; it is a pursuit that you enjoy and one which does not require you to compel others for any reason. If you pressurise anybody in order to indulge in your interests, then that interest degenerates into violence. Therefore, enjoy yourself blithely, indulging in all the pursuits which do not call upon you to exert pressure or compulsion upon others. Do not stop to consider whether others have deemed that particular pursuit as good or bad, and if required, become a bit obstinate in the matter of your hobbies. Pay scant heed to the critics, in fact, turn a deaf ear to other people's views on your hobbies; but yes, ensure that your hobbies are not hazardous to you in any way. If they are proving detrimental to you, then discard them with immediate effect. Otherwise, indulge in your hobbies with reckless abandon, whenever you can, for, the very moments indulged in hobbies are the ones where you experience ultimate freedom. This is verily the time when you are the emperor of your dreams and wishes, and experiencing these moments of pure, unadulterated joy, in turn, suffuses you with boundless energy. It wipes away every ounce of fatigue accumulated during the day, and lends you freshness and energy. Thus, be courageous, regardless of how twisted or complicated your life may be, and if needed, be a little brazen as well; there is nothing wrong in safeguarding your peace and joy. But do spend some time as per your wishes indulging in your hobbies, for, hobbies are your very lifeline and the principal reservoir of your energy.

Having said that, pray tell me, what do you do when you are tired of the daily grind? Why, you pack your bags and go on a holiday for a few days! And needless to say, you return completely refreshed and energised. Do you know why this is so? Because when you go on a holiday, you spend all your time fulfilling your wishes, breathing the air of freedom. And this is verily the point I am trying to convey; there is no greater source of energy than freedom. Thus, regardless of the worries and problems your life may be mired in, you need to allot some time to your hobbies. Bear in mind, you cannot ignore this important aspect of your life. For, living as per your wishes is a testament of you being alive, and for that matter, anyone who is leading his life as per the dictates of others cannot be called alive! Ergo, if you are alive and breathing, you should not only look alive but feel alive as well, and if you fail to do this least bit for yourself, you will forever remain weary and enervated. Thereafter, a feeling of enslavement will overwhelm you, and you will gradually slip into despondency, feeling helpless and impotent. Then, no task that you undertake will be discharged properly and your health will begin to deteriorate as well.

Therefore, I am urging you to be alive and look and feel alive as well. Gird up your loins, and do not throw up your hands in surrender even if your life seems twisted and tangled like a labyrinth on account of wrong influences. Under no circumstances must you lose out on the beautiful opportunity to live a splendid life, and for that purpose, make sure that you abound with energy at all times. For, only then will you be able to perform every task splendidly. Thus, rise from the ashes of your despair, open your eyes to a fresh perspective and be courageous. Make a staunch resolve to safeguard yourself in your own words. Regardless of how knotted your life may be, become an explorer who seeks new methods and ways to be alive and nurture his spirit, in defiance of his troubles. And if nothing else, at least ensure that you allocate one or two hours daily for spending time with yourself in the manner you wish, indulging only in pursuits that suffuse you with energy and grant you peace of mind. Be brave as well as brazen in order to fulfil this resolution. Regardless of the situation, be energised, full of life and raring to go. Irrespective of life's troubles and vexations, decide that you will in no way live a weary life, caught in the throes of compulsion and helplessness. So, without further ado, make a resolution in your own words, that you will safeguard yourself no matter what, breaking all the shackles that bind you, and throb with life, living it with joie de vivre once again. For that matter, this is your foremost duty towards yourself, so hold this close to your heart as the key *mantra* of your life. Now that I have explained the entire matter at length, the ball is in your court; hence, write your resolution succinctly, in your own words. Sum up whatever has made an impression on you in your own words, and contemplate over it on a regular basis.

Your *Mantra*

....

....

....

....

....

....

6. Stop squandering money on ostentation

Making grandiose and lofty declarations is quite easy, but they do not alter the ground reality, that in today's materialistic world, wealth has been exalted to the status of God. In fact, one requires wealth at every step of one's life, even if it is for charitable purposes; for, you cannot help another person simply by relying on God. Besides, in these contemporary times, it is wealth alone which is the primary necessity of the contractors and peddlers of religion, while all of the world's charitable trusts also remain engaged in trying to marshal wealth day in and day out. A large part of your life and that of your family also hinges upon wealth, and you certainly put in a lot of hard labour and sincerity in fending for yourself and your family. In that case, if you wish for your life to improve, you will have to diligently make efforts to break free from an age-old habit. You need to realise that this world is an illusion; the more you disregard it, the happier you will be. Ergo, do not squander your wealth in order to establish your status in the world; put the brakes on your profligate conduct and the ostentatious display of your wealth in order to impress others. Whether it is a house or a car, purchase it, but for your own enjoyment, and not with the intent to show off in front of others or in order to make others envious. Create a boundary for your life and function within its limits; make a firm resolution to invest in only those things which are best for you and are also well within your means. Your life, in reality, has nothing to do with other people's opinion of your status; ergo, kindly do not let yourself get caught in the illusory trap laid out by the world. A great number of people spend extravagantly in weddings in order to make an impression on society; pray tell me, what do they gain by such efforts? It is far better to observe austerity in your celebrations; instead, hold the wedding function at your home and splurge the money on yourself. The money saved would serve to fund several holidays for you and your family.

In a nutshell, you have earned your wealth by shedding blood, sweat and tears, so spend it only on the things which bring true happiness to you and your family. Do not squander it to pander to your ego; it is far better to use your wealth for noble purposes, for instance, in providing assistance to the needy rather than frittering it on your ego. I am certain everybody must have grasped this simple point. Obviously, those who have boundless wealth can do as they please with their wealth. But for the common man, it is best to use all their wealth for themselves and their near and dear ones. Thus, draft a staunch resolution for it in your own words. This one change will usher in unimaginable happiness in your life and that of your family, for, you have to live for yourself, not toil for your pretentious ego. Thus, bring about this change in yourself by writing down a firm resolution. This *mantra*, written by yourself, in your own words, will usher a remarkable transformation in your life. Hence, resolve that you will employ your wealth for personal happiness, not for gratifying your ego or for impressing others. Write this simple *mantra* in your own words and see how your life undergoes a sea change.

Your *Mantra*

....

....

....

....

....

....

....

....

7. Safeguarding yourself is your primary duty

Grandiose and vain teachings have all but ruined the world. We all are taught to serve others and this conditioning applies especially to women; it has been drilled into their psyche that they are born only to serve others, and must therefore spend their entire life tending to the needs of others. But the truth is, every human being, be it man or woman, throbs with life in equal measure, and all lives are equally precious. That is why, destroying oneself in order to save somebody else is the biggest folly one can commit, for, you are as precious as everybody else. Ergo, before attempting to save others, you must first safeguard yourself, for, if everyone takes care of themselves, nobody would need to sacrifice their happiness to care for others. However, this does not imply that you must refrain from helping others; helping as many people as one can, should certainly be the objective of human life. But the moot question to ask yourself before doing so is, who is actually capable of helping others? Well, the answer is simple, only a person who is truly alive and able. Hence, first and foremost, become truly alive and able yourself, and then serve the entire world. But do not commit the fallacy of saving others at the cost of your well-being. This will ascertain your ruin for sure, and you will not be able to save anybody else either. This is the reason I am impressing upon you to resolve that you will provide assistance and aid to others... only to the extent it does not lead to your own ruin. For, it is incumbent on everybody in this world to keep themselves alive, healthy and in good spirits. Why do you not grasp the simple fact that a sad and morose person can never be of assistance to anybody! So, do not go out of your way to the extent that you find yourself on the brink of ruination. Draw the line and retract from the point where you begin to cause damage to yourself. Lend a hand to your children, your parents, your family and also the society; do all that you can for them but only till the point where you do not start becoming a wreck yourself. You have to assist others only to the extent that it doesn't start affecting your own health and peace of mind. For, you are precious and it is imperative for you to be hale and hearty too. Besides, you will be able to help others only when you are yourself happy and healthy. Hence, protect yourself at all costs and ensure that your actions do not lead to your own destruction. For that matter, the ultimate principle of human psychology states that the extent to which a person will be able to help others is directly proportional to how alive he himself is. Interestingly, the lesson 'kill oneself to do good unto others' is drilled into people's minds only in order to exploit them. But neither must you sacrifice yourself nor let anyone in your family or community do anything which pushes them to the point of ruin. Live and let live: make this the ultimate principle of your life. By adopting this approach and diligently following it, your entire family will blossom, and happiness and joy will abound; but this can happen only when you bring this change in yourself. Whether it is your family or the world at large, speak up, put your foot down, but do not at any cost let anybody be subjected to oppression. As for yourself, resolve to not put your life on the line; safeguarding yourself will not only effect your betterment, but you will also be able to provide greater assistance to others. For my part, I have made a brief yet firm allusion; now, you must write down a firm and unwavering resolution for the same in your own words. This one resolution will cause an exponential surge in your happiness and that of your family. Therefore, resolve once and for all that you will not help anybody to the point of your own undoing. For that matter, if everyone in the world learns to take care of themselves, this world will invariably transform into a paradise.

Your *Mantra*

....

....

....

....

....

....

Core Essence of Step 1

Human life is verily a wonderful opportunity to live freely and wholeheartedly; it is a chance to accomplish feats of significance and prove your mettle. Ergo, a life so vital and beautiful cannot be allowed to be mired in the web of constraints and compulsions. Cloaking oneself in shrouds of failures, one cannot let this splendid opportunity go in vain. But the million-dollar question is, what must one do in order to make one's life beautiful? Well, there is only one answer to this; you must become your own doctor. For, this is Nature's *leela*, its design for human life. However, the greater majority of people entangle themselves in a multitude of futile solutions, rather than taking charge of their own life by becoming their own doctor. They seek all kinds of nugatory refuges and pay heed to nonsensical pronouncements in order to set their life on the path of progress. This leaves them rudderless, empty-handed and eventually, they have no option but to succumb to failures and compulsions. This act on their part is nothing but a kind of suicide; thus, one must simply refuse to accept any kind of refuge. Regardless of the situation, one must remain firm, standing on one's feet unflinchingly. I exhort you to brace yourself and decide once and for all that you will not live a submissive and lacklustre life, and once you make this decision, this book will automatically guide you on the path ahead.

Having said that, man's biggest predicament is, he wishes to set his life on the path of progress following the counsel of others. He wishes to thrive in life by placing his faith in others. And this sheer reliance on others is against the ultimate principle of Nature. Therefore, this book teaches you to become your own doctor and determine your dos and don'ts by yourself. For, one cannot prosper and progress in life without performing one's own surgery. So, imbibe all the practical applications given in the first step of this book deeply and thoroughly, and mould yourself into a completely new personality with their aid. Do not perceive this text as a book, no, this is your own great scripture, an invaluable guide that you are penning yourself; hence, it is certain to produce a lasting impact. You must apprehend that the mere act of breathing in and out is not a testimony of you being alive; only a person whose life is manifesting as per his wishes, in whose life everything is transpiring as per his wishes, can be called truly alive. A person who is at the helm of his life, someone who is free and unfazed like the wild wind, who is blithe and merry like a burst of spring, and who abounds with unbridled energy to perform his duties and responsibilities can be called truly alive. Everybody else is just a breathing corpse, wandering aimlessly in a state of unawareness. Therefore, you must become truly alive, and in order to do so, you must become your own doctor and resolutely imbibe and implement all the practical applications provided in step 1. Thereafter, with their guidance and assistance, you must perform a precise surgery of yourself, the successful execution of which will reward you with a personality that would be far more impressive than ever before. Furthermore, your life will make great strides on the path of progress, powered by heightened energy and enhanced self-confidence, while all your confusions regarding life will disappear. Most importantly, you will taste the sweet nectar of freedom, experience its unbridled passion like never before, and be liberated from the bondage of countless absurd enslavements.

A word to the wise... do not be the least bit hasty, write down each one of your resolutions calmly and resolutely. Let every resolution you pen become an inextricable part of your existence; for, when you have frittered away so many years in employing nonsensical solutions, a little more time spent in reflecting on the right path will not make much of a difference. But, come what may, imbibe and implement all the practical applications provided in step 1, weaving them seamlessly into your personality, thus, making them a natural part of your personality; this will overnight effect a remarkable transformation into your life. And only when this comes to pass, should you consider yourself capable and prepared to embark on step 2. Moving further, we shall certainly proceed with the practical applications of step 2, which will undoubtedly banish all your sufferings and miseries. But only a person who has thoroughly imbibed step 1 will be able to benefit from step 2. In other words, the effective result of the practical applications of step 2 will reflect only on your new and reformed personality. Hence, do not be in a hurry to jump to step 2; first instate yourself firmly in step 1. Besides, as you are all sensible people desirous of a glorious life, it will not take you very long to enhance your personality. On this note, let us proceed to step 2, which will expel your sorrows and suffering from its root and instate you on the zenith of joy, energy and peace. All you have to do is be guided by it, and behold how this scripture composed by you transcends your life to unimaginable heights.

STEP 2

I shall now proceed on the assumption that everybody has assuredly passed the examination of step 1 with flying colours. As you are penning your own scripture, it is a given that it is you who has to prepare the question paper and subsequently, examine it and award yourself with a grade too. We are moving towards a realm where 'you' alone are your entire world, and besides, this is verily the truth of life as well. Having said that, let me reiterate, if for some reason, you feel you have not been able to imbibe all the learnings of step 1 and are still on shaky ground, then I implore you, halt where you are and focus on instating yourself in step 1 thoroughly; do not be in a hurry to proceed further. This book is your very own scripture and it shall invariably remain with you; so before you proceed, imbibe the learnings of step 1 properly and let its practical applications seep within you so that they become an inseparable part of your personality. For, without clearing step 1, you will not be able to derive much practical benefit out of step 2. Ergo, in order to elevate your life to greater heights, you must first clear step 1 with remarkable results.

As we proceed to step 2, let me commence this discussion with asking you a simple question. What do you think is the gravest problem a human being is plagued with? As you are all intelligent and thinking beings, give this question a little thought and only then, provide me with the answer. Verily, it has to do with your own life, so you must assuredly know the answer, and I am certain the majority of people are already aware of the answer. Moreover, I am here to lend you assistance with regard to the aspects that require clarification. The obvious answer to this question is, your sorrows are the biggest problem haunting your life; the tensions gripping you are the cause of your agitation, while the fears plaguing you round the clock constitute your trouble. Your frustration vexes you, whereas scores of unfulfilled wishes and untold heartbreaks fill you with disquiet. To be rid of all the above problems is just what everybody wishes for. Besides, these problems are not a new phenomenon or a product of the present time; they have been hounding man since time immemorial. Moreover, it would be erroneous to state that only a handful of people are perturbed by these worries; for, almost all of mankind has fallen prey to these problems. Day in and day out, everybody is striving to break the shackles they are bound in, and free themselves from the formidable clutches of these problems. So, this begs the question, why do miseries and tribulations still rear their ugly heads in human lives despite tireless efforts on the part of each one of us? I do not think there is any other question more vital to man than this. Just imagine, what an Elysian world one would live in, if life was bereft of negativity; a world where pain, sorrow, tension, fear and frustration are barred from even touching it! Life would then be suffused with the vibrant hues of joy and cheer as they would abound your world and pervade your entire being with freedom and bliss. But unfortunately, nobody is able to give a thought to this matter, for, everyone is afflicted by problems. To be honest, this is the reason everyone has accepted sorrow as life's unavoidable companion. However, this laying down of arms and complete surrender of man to his problems is simply unacceptable to me. Life is the ultimate opportunity granted by Nature; so how can one spend one's life suffering the torment of pain, sorrow and frustration? Surely, this is not acceptable. Hence, we will conduct a complete psychoanalysis of this subject and be liberated of these problems once and for all.

There is no denying that everyone wants to be liberated of pains and sorrows, and everyone endeavours indefatigably to this end. But to solve their problems, people are perpetually following the dictates of others who don the cloak of advisors and guides, and this is where they falter. It is vital to comprehend here, that nobody is trying to put an end to pains and sorrows as per their own comprehension; instead they are all trying their hand at solutions offered to them by others. If someone advocates, 'Believe in God, for, he alone will dispel all your pains and sorrows,' everyone starts believing in God and worshipping him blindly. And, trust me, if you cast a glance around, the realisation will dawn on you that this nugatory practice has been prevalent for centuries together. Even in today's scientific age, there will be, at the most, only ten percent of the population which harbours the belief that God cannot obliterate all their problems. Everybody else is visiting holy places, making a big pomp and show in an effort to appease their respective gods. But even after indulging in all these acts, miseries and sorrows, instead of diminishing, are multiplying drastically. Akin to a puppet being pulled on strings, you are then instructed to change your god, and you happily oblige; while on someone else's advice, you resort to a different approach just as quickly. But despite following every possible instruction, miseries and sorrows refuse to abate. Ironically, despite such measures proving to be abysmal failures, people still resort to these solutions.

And they will continue to prevail, because now, you are joined on this trail by the holy men who profess that God does not relieve one of pains and sorrows for free. God needs to be worshipped according to what is delineated in the religious scriptures such as the Vedas, Quran and Bible, to serve that purpose. Only then does God dispel your tensions, fears and frustrations. Thereafter, a human being starts demonstrating ever more startling antics. He eats as per the instructions outlined in these scriptures, he conducts worship only as per the methods suggested by them, and he starts observing fasts and follows every letter written in the scriptures with unwavering fervour and devotion. Interestingly, the world is teeming with not just a handful but hundreds and thousands of scriptures. Furthermore, all these scriptures are at variance with one another, mentioning diametrically opposite ideas. Thus, that which is included in the list of dos in one scripture, is considered a grave sin as per another scripture; notwithstanding this, man continues to perform a variety of antics. But alas, sorrow, tension, frustration and pains perversely refuse to abate. And unfortunately, even after barely scraping to survive in this bleak scenario, good sense does not prevail and everybody continues with their antics without a change in the tempo.

Thereafter, a few more pseudo-intellectuals jump into the fray, who take great pains and efforts to explain to you that your belief in God is all very well, but if you wish to set your life on the path of progress, then education is imperative. 'All right' one thinks, 'let me obtain a good education; perhaps bright and pristine academic degrees will banish the sorrows and miseries plaguing my life.' Thereafter, many go ahead and secure an educational degree, but pains and sorrows continue dogging their footsteps. Somebody else then declares in honey-laced tones, 'Is this the way to banish troubles and sufferings from life? Certainly not! Can miseries and sorrows ever be made to disappear in this manner? What you must focus on is amassing wealth and becoming a man of consequence...then you can flick away the troubles and miseries thronging your life at the snap of a finger.' No sooner you hear this than you jump into the mad race of securing wealth and riches with the belief that once you have a formidable collection of material possessions to your name, sorrows and miseries will stand no chance of tormenting you. Then, you leave no stone unturned in this endeavour, and interestingly, some people do succeed in this venture and become wealthy and affluent too. But even so, there is no change in the status quo; one fails to be liberated from sorrows and miseries. During this phase of struggle and strife, one even goes ahead and ties the knot, procreates, and yet, pains and sorrows remain his constant companions, multiplying at a furious pace. If I were to state this differently, everybody is engaged in trying out all possible solutions, but nobody's pains and sorrows are ever dispelled, or for that matter, even diminished. Despite this, nobody gives this a serious thought or tries to dig at the root of this problem. Everybody is manically engaged in employing one solution after another akin to a robot, and ultimately, one day, spent out and weary, they bid adieu to this world. It wrenches at the heart to watch man endure such burden of hardship and struggle all through his life... and in the end, depart from this world in a state of absolute restlessness. How can one bear to see a human being languish in such a deplorable state; a human being who is, after all, the ultimate creation of Nature! The sight is certainly heartbreaking!

This brings us to the question, can a human being's pains and sorrows never be cast away? Of course, they can and quite easily, if you heed the practical applications I have listed below. History bears witness to the fact that many great people have verily vanquished troubles and hardships, and you too must certainly add your name to the hallowed hall of fame alongside these stalwarts. Indeed, this exercise will prove to be effortless for the one who has properly imbibed step 1, because he will easily comprehend that solutions such as God, religion, scriptures, society, academic degrees, spouse, children and wealth have been forced upon you by others. And as per Nature's design, the solutions proffered by others will never be able to banish your life's woes and troubles. To give you an example, Arjuna had also found himself despondent, prior to the battle of Mahabharata. And he too had wished to rid himself of misery, by engaging in a dialogue with Krishna about religion, scriptures, morality, society, kingdom and virtue-sin. Furthermore, he had relentlessly provided rationalisations and justifications to Krishna in favour of these recourses. But Krishna had made it expressly clear to Arjuna that such borrowed knowledge could never help to rid him of woes and troubles, and that the latter would have to kindle his own understanding in order to chase away his troubles. Most importantly, Krishna offered to help Arjuna awaken his own intelligence. And five thousand years later, I too am urging you to do the same; I am not disclosing any new ideas to you; it is only the manner of expression and approach that has taken a scientific tone. Simply stated, you can bid adieu to your pains and sorrows and the tensions and frustrations plaguing you, if you show the door to the solutions provided by others and awaken your own intelligence. And if you are able to kindle the fire within you and be receptive, I can provide you truly wonderful assistance in this regard, but everything will be in vain if borrowed solutions prevail over you even at present. However, I am certain, you will not let this happen, for, you are sure to comprehend the simple truth that your life cannot be freed from the shackles of troubles and miseries by following the solutions, which millions and billions of people have already attempted but with little success. And this realisation will effortlessly dawn on you if you have, indeed, thoroughly imbibed step 1. I believe you do not wish to let your life go in vain, and you assuredly wish to be liberated of all kinds of tensions and frustrations. Nursing the hope that you will cast out everything old and embrace a new and scientific approach to that end, I shall now proceed further.

Now, the first point you must comprehend in this context is, two types of pronouncements are prevalent in the human world; one, human declarations which connect deliverance from sorrows and miseries with religion, scriptures, society, education, wealth, splendour and so on. All such pronouncements are a product of the human brain and establishing any direct connection between them and man's deliverance from miseries and sorrows is well-nigh impossible, because these are completely at variance with Nature's fundamental design. But this does not mean that they are all worthless; good health, education, glory and family, are all mighty fine things to possess, but they cannot liberate you from your woes and sorrows. If you need substantiation of this fact, then cast a glance around you. You must have seen people with humungous amount of wealth who are (surprisingly) frustrated with their lives, as well as disturbed and distressed religious *gurus*. Neither men of letters nor those born with a silver spoon are free from woes and worries. So, it is high time you comprehend the simple truth that all of these human-generated pronouncements have no connection whatsoever with deliverance from sorrows and miseries. The appearance and disappearance of sorrow, anguish, tension and fear in human life has its own natural reasons, without grasping which, grief and hardships can never be cast out from human life. Having said that, pains and sorrows must be dispelled from life at any cost, for, to live a grief-stricken life is to lose out on a great opportunity. Man is the most beautiful creation of Nature simply because he is the only one who can be happy and blissful, who can be infinitely creative and who can scale ever new heights of success. But all this is possible only when life is free of grief and sorrows. Sorrow and happiness cannot co-exist, and it naturally follows then that a scared and anxious person can never be blithe and merry. Thus, instead of ruminating over how to coax happiness into your life, reflect on how to oust sorrows and hardships. When sorrows and tensions will no longer rear their ugly heads in your life, what will remain will verily be pure happiness. And you ought to spend your life with a smile on your face and a song in your heart, else it will be an utter disgrace to the human life you have been bestowed with. For, you are the only one with access to all these opportunities; neither can the moon and stars sing and dance nor are the animals capable of extraordinary creativity. It is only you who have been blessed with this opportunity. However, if you still squander your life, bemoaning and wringing your hands in despair, then I have no words left to explain anything to you on this matter.

Having said that, I am aware that it would perhaps not be easy for everyone to imbibe all these instructions immediately, but for those who have assimilated the learnings of step 1, it is not a herculean task either. And, you are doubtless one of them, so let us proceed to comprehending which solution has a direct connection with the deliverance of human beings from woes and sorrows. And in this context, I have already mentioned that Nature's design is verily the ultimate authority of human life; there is nothing above or beyond it. If you wish to decipher the laws of Nature in their entirety, then read my upcoming book 'The Laws of Nature'. Post reading this book, the entire design of Nature will become crystal clear to you. For now, the important point to comprehend is, as the laws of Nature are the ultimate authority of this world, all human teachings and pronouncements pale in comparison and prove abysmal failures in validating themselves time and again. But unfortunately, their appeal is so alluring that people are inexorably drawn towards them. Besides, what can a man possibly do? For, there is scarce knowledge available on the subject of Nature's powers and nobody knows much about them either. But if you have noted, all my statements revolve around Nature's powers; ergo, there are instantaneous benefits of tapping into them.

Now, I will forthwith speak of the ultimate design of Nature and with its support, I will continue the discussion on how to dispel one's sorrows and miseries for good. In Nature's scheme of things, man is ultimately the mind; his very core essence is nothing but the mind. And what is the mind? A gust of sweet emotions and a storehouse of incredible powers. You are simply this, and your entire existence is encapsulated in this definition...and since this is Nature's design for you, it is absolute. The moment you step beyond this point, you will land yourself in grave trouble and doubtless pay a hefty price in the form of pains and sorrows. In the same vein, Nature's second design for you is the body and intelligence provided to you in order to manifest your mind's powers. In simpler terms, you are only a mind wherein positive emotions such as joy, merriment, peace and so on perpetually flow. At the same time, powers like concentration, enthusiasm and self-confidence also dwell in you, that is, in your mind, and this verily is your pure existence bestowed by Nature. As per Nature's design, tasks continuously spring forth in an unending stream from the mind through the means of the mind's powers like self-confidence, concentration and enthusiasm, and every time you engage in any such task, you experience joy, peace and merriment. This is verily your pure existence and the right way of undertaking tasks, as prescribed by Nature. But there is a twist here; despite the indomitable power of the mind to achieve unimaginable feats, it is not vested with the power to execute tasks. And for that very purpose, Nature has provided man with body and brain. In other words, tasks must germinate and emerge from the mind, and then the body and brain must together execute those tasks; this is the only way of existence for a human being. And verily, this is how Nature has designed a human being. Here, you must also comprehend that Nature has begotten man only with his powerful minds, therefore, when I speak of the mind, I am speaking only of the powerful minds. To summarise, sorrow, worry, fear and frustration can never invade one's life if one follows this design of Nature. It is only on account of his brain that man has transgressed this design of Nature; impudent, he abuses the intelligence granted to him. And this is verily the root cause of all his sorrows and failures. Now certainly, this matter is profound, so it is quite possible that you might fail to comprehend it all at once. Never mind! It does not matter if you are unable to comprehend it at once, read it repeatedly, over and over again, to apprehend it in its entirety. Besides, I will also explain it in detail as we proceed further. For now, just imbed in your mind that man's transgression of Nature's design is verily the root cause of all his sorrows.

Now, what does transgression of Nature's design imply? I am certain this question must be badgering everyone even now. So, without further ado, let me reveal the answer to this question, and in that context, note once again quite clearly that according to Nature's design, tasks had to spring forth from the mind, while the body and the brain are the instruments through which those tasks were to be implemented. And only if this system is upheld, pains and sorrows will not sneak into one's life. But owing to baseless instructions and incorrect teachings, everything has turned topsy-turvy; rather than implementing the tasks kindling from the mind, man's brain has assumed authority and started making decisions concerning the said tasks. In other words, the brain has started determining the tasks that should or should not be undertaken. Furthermore, the brain has assumed control over the body as well, leading to the advent of pains and sorrows in man's life. This change in hierarchy has made the brain and the body masters of the system, which were provided by Nature in order to carry out the wishes of man's powerful minds. And it is from this point that everybody's lives have started spiralling into darkness. For, no sooner did it hold the master's whip in its hands than the brain created the weaker minds, whose wont was to establish connection with the external world; and it is verily these weak minds which are the biggest problem. Well, if you wish to comprehend this entire science of the mind in greater detail, you must read my book 'I am the Mind'. For now, just comprehend that you have foolishly provided the servants an opportunity to become the masters of a company that you were the sole owner of. And now you are in a muddle, caught in a situation where you have one car, but it is being steered by two drivers, and both these drivers are completely at variance with each other. This has engendered absolute confusion and chaos, as the drivers are manoeuvring the life's car in opposite directions, thus, creating a perfect recipe for disaster and recurring accidents in life. And naturally, when accidents occur with such an alarming frequency, what else can you expect besides pain and sorrow? As a result, life has been enmeshed in a series of pains and troubles. Furthermore, not only a few people but the greater majority of mankind has become ensnared in this tenacious web. This is the only reason why everyone's lives have become fraught with pains and sorrows; else there is really no other reason for misery and sorrows to prevail in human life. Now, this is a simple matter, but you might still find it difficult to comprehend, because there is an overabundance of ignorance in this world and the greater part of human race has fallen prey to this ignorance. Hence, it can certainly seem difficult to comprehend this profound design of Nature. However, I am here to render assistance and that is why, I am elucidating everything in the simplest of language, offering a step-by-step approach. All you have to do is, read and assimilate all that has been stated, over and over again, in case you fail to grasp it in one reading. At present, in order to aid your comprehension, I shall explain the difference between the working methodologies of the brain and the mind, by means of a chart. For, the majority of people are oblivious to this difference, and this will certainly make it easier for you to grasp the point I have been trying to drive home.

Working Methodology of the Powerful Minds	Working Methodology of the Weak Minds and Brain
1. The world of the mind begins and ends with itself.	1. The entire world of the brain lies outside.
2. The mind is not overly influenced by the events occurring in the external world.	2. The brain has a deep interest in every activity taking place in the external world.
3. The tasks of the mind spring forth spontaneously, from within. The mind has no interest in the reasons behind or outcomes of those tasks.	3. The brain determines its tasks on the basis of duality such as good-bad or right-wrong. Reason and outcome are at the core of its every task.
4. The mind is completely focused in a single direction and is unwavering on its path. Thus, it remains absorbed entirely in the task.	4. As the brain decides to undertake tasks on the basis of duality, it consequently expects gain, victory and everything that is desirable as an outcome.
5. The mind derives pleasure from the task. Neither is it interested in its outcome nor is it influenced by it. In other words, the mind undertakes a task only for the enjoyment it begets. It yearns for only peace.	5. The brain does not mind enduring sorrow and hardship, if it derives worldly progress in exchange.
6. The mind does not consider even the body and the brain as its own; it views them only as slaves, meant for implementing its ardent pursuits.	6. The brain is invariably attracted not only to the body but the charm and dazzle of the entire world, and consequently, it wishes to acquire as many external, materialistic objects as it can.

7. In summation, the mind barely has any connection with the external world.	7. The brain remains completely connected with everything that belongs to the external world.

On the basis of this chart, assess yourself in all honesty; you will indubitably find the brain reigning supreme over your life at present. But this certainly does not imply that the mind is suppressed for good, for, even today, the desire for joy, peace and harmony must still be alive within you. The only difference is, the one who nurtures a greater desire for peace and harmony should comprehend that his mind is still strong, whereas the person who wishes for worldly possessions at the cost of hardships and struggles must apprehend that the brain has established complete ascendancy over his life. However, since both are alive and kicking, everyone is oscillating from one end to the other like the veritable pendulum of a clock, and that is why, everyone remains in a constant state of delusion. The greater majority of people in the world aspire for both peace as well as worldly possessions. Now, this in turn, gives rise to many questions. The first being, should one attain peace first or make a run for worldly achievements first? Secondly, can both peace and possessions not be attained simultaneously? Well, before answering these questions, I will shed light on a few brief points, which will make it easier for you to comprehend this profound matter.

A) First and foremost, you are only the mind, hence you cannot completely stifle the wishes of the mind. And what does the mind wish for? Only...to live in joy, merriment and tranquillity. And that is why, it is well-nigh impossible to find a human being who would relinquish his desire for happiness, enjoyment, peace and harmony. Moreover, the brain, for its part, is fully cognisant of this strong desire of the mind, and that is why, it contrives reasons to trick the mind. The reasoning it provides to the mind is, how can one attain joy, peace, harmony and so on, without religion, society, family, wealth and glory? By voicing the concerns and contention of everyone, right from religion to family, it lures the mind, and the mind is thus enticed into the lair. If you give this matter careful thought, you will apprehend that you have also been beguiled in the same manner. You too have come to accept that one cannot enjoy life in the absence of religion, society, family, wealth, and so on. But let me clarify here that both, the people who make such assertions and those who believe them to be true, are sadly mistaken. And one need not go further to substantiate this fact; most of the above-mentioned aspects, be it religion or family, are part of everybody's lives. However, despite being in the possession of so many things, just pause and think for a moment, is your life really joyous and peaceful? Have sorrows and tensions receded from your life? Well, we are all quite cognisant of the answer! Therefore, first of all, apprehend the truth that religion, society, wealth and family have no particular connection with peace and harmony. And no sooner you evoke this understanding than you will automatically attain a great victory.

B) Let us proceed to the second point now. Can you tell me, which is the most wonderful phase of human life? I am certain the majority of people will state that it is their childhood. Look, how easily you have admitted such a profound truth, all by yourself. Now, tell me, what was it that made your childhood so wonderful? Well, your childhood days were the happiest days of your life, because negative emotions like worry, fear, frustration and sorrow had no place in it. And do you know why this was so? It is because a child lives his life comfortably ensconced in his powerful minds; he is totally devoid of any conception of religion, God, scriptures, society, education, wealth and glory. In other words, he is free from the illusory trap of the brain, and consequently, his life abounds with joy, peace and harmony. Nestled in this safe haven, he lives his life with such abandon that the entire world becomes enamoured of him. Tell me, honestly, can any person claim that he is not entranced by the innocence and unrestrained joy that children dwell in? This directly establishes the fact that man's enjoyment, peace and harmony are not dependent on any external factor, and all kinds of external dependencies are verily the root cause of all of man's sorrows. Furthermore, it has also been conclusively proven that all 'knowledge', right from religion to society, is simply an extension of the illusory trap of the brain and this is precisely the reason why, a person ensnared by them forfeits his peace and happiness. And verily, the happy-go-lucky life of children bears testimony to this truth. Hence, the second point you must etch in your mind is, man's happiness has no connection whatsoever with anything external, for, everybody has indubitably led a memorable childhood, even though they had nothing to their name in those days.

C) Now, you might say, 'We have comprehended that man's happiness and peace are not dependent on anything external, and that the illusory trap laid down by the brain is at the root of all of man's sorrows. But what is wrong with progressing in life and attaining wealth and glory?' Why, absolutely nothing at all! In fact, to attain material possessions and to derive the utmost enjoyment from them is verily the goal of human life. But you must comprehend that the brain cannot help you attain all of this; had it been capable enough, sorrows and failures would have dissipated from your life forever. To substantiate my statement, I urge you to keenly cast a glance around you. The greater part of mankind is ensnared in the illusory trap of the brain. Everybody is in possession of everything, right from religion and scriptures to society and family, and everyone is invariably engaged in the mad race to attain everything. But tell me, how many of these people have attained wealth and glory? Moreover, the brain extracts a hefty price in the form of hardships and struggle for whatever little it lets you obtain. In other words, whatever little you gain by employing your brain, you do so by forsaking your happiness and peace. Therefore, this method of attaining material success in life is essentially wrong, and for that matter, attaining anything at the cost of one's happiness and peace of mind is, indeed, a loss-making proposition. That is why, to wish for wealth and to actually be wealthy are two entirely different matters. It is, indeed, true that one cannot attain glory just by wishing for it, but at the same time, it is also a fact that a profusion of sorrows barge into your life as soon as you become a part of the worldly race. In other words, by doing this, you will forfeit both material success and also your happiness and peace. In conclusion, all knowledge prescribed by the brain is eventually doing nothing save for leading one astray.

D) This being the case, you would be justified to ask, 'What should one do then? For, we all aspire for happiness and peace as well as prosperity and grandeur.' Well, it is my wish too, to see you all progress in both aspects of life, and it is for that very purpose that I am establishing such an extensive and solid foundation. You might very well ask, 'Is it really possible to attain progress in life without sacrificing one's happiness and peace? Can one, indeed, scale the heights of wealth and grandeur while still being instated in happiness and joy?' Of course, one can! This is fairly easy with the aid of one's powerful minds. For, the mind is connected with Nature and that is precisely why, it goes on performing miracles easily and effortlessly. This is verily Nature's *leela*, its play, and in this *leela* of Nature, there is simply no need to sacrifice one's happiness and peace in order to attain worldly success. At the same time, the mind and Nature are not bound by worldly constraints; they can lift man from the nadir of his circumstances and elevate him to greatness. And you too must have observed that the preponderance of great people hail from impoverished backgrounds, and by and large, they are not very well educated either; many amongst them are atheists as well. Even so, overcoming all obstacles, they do attain happiness, blithely and effortlessly. But the brain, failing to comprehend this, connects this simple matter with concepts such as action *(karma)* and its fruit as well as destiny. Nevertheless, these are all miracles effected through the union of the mind and Nature, which can perch even an ordinary human being on the pinnacle of success.

I have, with the help of the four points mentioned above, tried to explain Nature's design, and have also cautioned you regarding the brain's illusory trap. Having comprehended this thoroughly, you must have found the answers to both your questions as well. Furthermore, you would have discerned the fact that your powerful minds can easily and effortlessly lead you to worldly achievements; in other words, you can doubtless attain both success and peace at the same time. But you must fulfil one condition in order to materialise this; the brain and the body should remain servile to the mind; if perchance these two become the masters, you will end up forfeiting both happiness as well as material success. So far, we have comprehended that one can attain both inner peace and material success simultaneously, by honouring the design of Nature. But what about those unfortunate people, who have lost out on both peace and success, by according their brain the authority to become their master? Yes, indeed... I will elaborate on that point too, for, I am well acquainted with the fact that the majority of people have squandered away both their peace as well as success. But there is no need for such people to be disappointed either; because step 2 and step 3 are designed for this very purpose. We will dispel our sorrows and miseries with the aid of step 2, while step 3 will help us set off on a great flight to success. In other words, even if we have strayed away from the right track, we will assuredly attain both, gradually, one after the other. Now, had you stuck to the right path since childhood, you would have easily attained both peace and success. But, despair not; all is not lost yet, you will certainly attain both success and happiness even now. This book is penned for that very purpose and that is the only reason I am imploring you to compose your own scripture. In this regard, you must clearly comprehend, once the illusory trap of the brain is shattered, and the scales weighing you down are lifted, you will become a pure mind once again. And once you become a pure mind, devoid of pains and miseries in step 2, we will discuss how to blithely and effortlessly scale the ladder of success in step 3.

From our discussion so far, we have comprehended clearly that we are entrapped, and we will first have to regain our peace of mind. We have also learnt that as long as there are pains and miseries, our life cannot soar to great heights. We also know that no sooner we become a pure mind devoid of pains and miseries than success will come knocking at our door. But the question is, will it be so easy to banish pains and sorrows from life?

Obviously not! Especially, when one is so entangled in the illusory trap of the brain. However, fret not and do not give up hope.

If you have properly imbibed step 1, you will not find this process difficult. For, step 1 teaches you to assume ownership of your life, lessening the pressures of the world and granting you freedom. And if you have been truly freed of the chains that bind you, you can easily perform the surgical operation provided in step 2 and swiftly break free from the shackles of pains and sorrows. However, you have to continue being your own doctor even in step 2. In other words, you have to bear in mind Nature's design at every step of the way. Thereafter, when you dispel your pains and sorrows upon clearing this step, you will enter step 3, where we will learn how to advance in life, merrily and effortlessly, with the help of a pure mind. But prior to that, you need to banish pains and sorrows from your life. For, the elimination of pains and sorrows from life is, in itself, an incredible achievement. And once this comes to pass, you will invariably ascend the steps of success, joyfully and effortlessly.

With this, I hope you have girded up your loins to dispel sorrows and miseries from life. You must comprehend once and for all that there is no other way to oust sorrows and miseries other than diligently following the step 2 detailed in this book. For, sorrows and miseries will inevitably plague a person who misses this step, and it is well-nigh impossible to attain success while shouldering the gruelling burden of pains and sorrows. Moreover, the biggest fallout of not following step 2 would be, you will simply fail to imbibe step 3. Thus, you must categorically conceive all the superficial and fantastical statements that claim to dispel sorrows and miseries as nothing but a tall tale; indeed, I am making such a big assertion because what I am stating is both natural as well as scientific. For, if you miss this chance of ousting sorrows and miseries from your life, hardships and troubles will continue to haunt you till you breathe your last. So, with the belief that I will receive your full cooperation in this endeavour of mine, I shall now proceed further. Bear in mind, never again will you find such a scientific method to cast out sorrows and miseries from life.

Well, you have very well comprehended that in order to liberate oneself from pains and hardships, one will have to become a pure and pellucid mind once again. So, let us now apprehend what it means to be a pure mind. The greatest speciality of a pure mind is, it is completely free; and since you are nothing but a pure mind, you too are completely free. In other words, as far as Nature is concerned, it has sent every human being into this world with complete freedom, and when a human being's mind is wholly free, then it simply implies that nothing, save for his own mind, can make him sad and miserable. Not destiny, not God, not religion nor Nature; if anybody can make a person woeful and despondent, then it is he himself. For, establishing a connection with the external world is at the root of all sorrows, and a human being has himself established these connections; nobody has compelled him to do so. Consequently, he cannot hold anybody else the least bit responsible for it. Hence, you must etch this truth in your mind for good, for, it is this truth which will prove most helpful in order to eliminate hardships and sorrows.

Possibly, you might not have comprehended this matter in its entirety, for in the present time, it has become difficult to apprehend that the human mind is completely free. Mired in ignorance, everybody has cloaked themselves in so many bondages that it has become impossible to digest the fact that one can be completely free. Therefore, let me try to explain this matter with an example from the life of Alexander the Great. This incident dates back to the time when, having conquered the north-western province of India, he was preparing to return to Greece with his carts laden with heaps of treasure. Suddenly, the thought struck him, 'When I am taking so much treasure from India with me, why not take a *sanyasi* (saint) along as well; after all, Indian *sanyasis* are also quite famous.' No sooner did he decide this than he ordered his soldiers to catch hold of a *sanyasi* and bring the saint to him. In a short while, the soldiers, obeying their king's command, brought a *sanyasi* before him, by the name of Dandyayan. As soon as the saint was presented before Alexander, the saint asked him the reason for his detention without a valid reason.

Alexander answered, "Fear not! You haven't been detained. You have been brought here with the sole intent to be taken to Greece with me with all due respect and courtesy, so that the people of my country can make the acquaintance of an Indian saint."

Dandyayan remarked, "That is all very well but I have no wish to go to Greece."

Alexander replied, "Perhaps you are not aware that I revere *sanyasis* and *fakirs*. Not only will you be respected there but I will also establish a magnificent school for you in Greece."

Dandyayan answered, "O King of Greece! Do not try to tempt me with greed. *Sanyasis* cannot be won over by greed. I will not go to Greece and that is my final word."

Alexander laughed at the arrogance of the *sanyasi* and said, "Listen, I have conquered the entire world. There is nobody who can stop me... So, when I have decided that you have to accompany me to my homeland, then come you must. And when you have to accompany me, it is better that you do so happily and agreeably."

Dandyayan retorted, "O King, conquering a country and plundering treasure is nowhere near as difficult as making a *sanyasi* go anywhere against his will. You cannot forcibly take me with you."

Hearing the *sanyasi* make such an assertion, Alexander, who was intoxicated on his scores of victories and unmatchable power, guffawed and roaring with laughter, he declared, "What nonsense! Who will stop me...? I will make your arrogance bite the dust this very moment." Saying so, he ordered his soldiers to bind the *sanyasi* and force him into a chariot. The order was carried out with immediate effect and the *sanyasi* was bound and put in a chariot. As soon as he was bound, Alexander came and stood before him. And a trifle haughtily, he asked, "Do you still think that I cannot take you along?"

Dandyayan replied, "Yes...you cannot."

"How can that be?" Alexander asked incredulously.

Dandyayan replied, "You have bound my body and you can certainly exert force on it, but do you want my body or my saintly consciousness? If you want my consciousness, then it is under my control and it is well-nigh impossible to take it. Upon reaching Greece, it will go silent. Then, you will be merely left with my body. Tell me, of what use would that be to you?"

Alexander was rendered speechless upon hearing Dandyayan's words. He immediately apologised to the saint and set him free. He realised that vanquishing kings and plundering treasure was easy, but making a true saint go anywhere against his will or winning him over was no mean feat.

After reading this story, I hope you must have grasped that despite all his might, Alexander could not turn the *sanyasi* into a slave even for a moment. Pertinently, the same is the case with your mind; others can bind your body or exert force over it, but no power on earth can assume control over your mind. One can bind you and ask you to shower praises upon him, and you might even mouth honey-laced words, but in your mind, you are at liberty to rain curses on him. In simple words, nobody can prevail over your mind without your consent, and when nobody can assume control over it, then, it implies, nobody, without your permission, can make you miserable either. Thus, if you, indeed, wish to dispel sorrows and miseries from your life, you will, first and foremost, have to consider yourself responsible for the same. You will have to stop laying the blame of your despondency on others... be it family, religion, destiny, society, God and action (*karma*) and its fruits... You will have to take ownership of your actions and accept that nothing and nobody except you is to be blamed; if you are aggrieved and sorrowful, then it is solely you who is at fault; for that matter, the person who is completely free to act can simply not hold other people culpable for his own insensible acts. Ergo, you yourself are responsible for your pains and sorrows and you must shoulder this responsibility yourself. Now, let us come straight to how you can get rid of your pains and sorrows for good by assuming this responsibility, for, I believe, you are no longer confused with regard to the complete freedom of your mind. And when you are completely free, you must have also comprehended that you cannot hold others responsible for your sorrows. Hence, without further ado, let us forge ahead and purge all kinds of negative emotions from our mind. We will systematically imbibe the practical applications of step 2, and be liberated of all pains and sorrows. I am confident that you are all eager and ready to take this giant leap, and to this effect, I will discuss one negative emotion after the other, and simultaneously provide you with practical applications to find release from that particular emotion. All you must do is derive the utmost benefit from every practical application being provided, and come what may, liberate yourself from all your pains and sorrows for good.

A) Chase Away Your Sorrows

Generally, every person succumbs to sorrow at one point or another in his life. Nobody in this world has been able to escape its snare; at some point in our life, in lesser or greater degree, we have all invariably experienced sorrow. And we are also cognisant of the great trouble and vexation that sorrow brings in its wake. A person may be blessed with everything in life, but if he is stricken by sorrow, a dark shroud of gloom is cast over his life, as he wriggles and writhes in it for days and months. Having said this, it is also a fact that nobody has invited sorrow in their life on purpose. This begs the question, where does it appear from? How does this uninvited, dangerous guest force its entry into your mind? Have you ever pondered over this? When you do not let anybody step into your car without your express permission, how is it that sorrow enters your mind effortlessly, especially considering the fact that your mind is far more precious to you? How does sorrow barge into your mind against your wishes? Why do you never reflect on this matter when you know well that sorrow causes you such grave distress? Isn't it incredible that you never give a thought to something which begets such pain in your life? On what grounds do you proclaim then that your life is most valuable to you? Besides, if you ever think carefully about it, your thoughts border on the ridiculous and nonsensical. You cherish the notion that you will be delivered from sorrows by observing fasts. Or, perhaps, you think that amassing heaps of wealth or pandering to popular ideas will liberate you from the shackles of sorrow. Well, thinking along these lines, indeed, reflects the height of psychological ignorance on your part. None of these measures is the least bit effective in banishing life's sorrows and miseries. On the contrary, such futile solutions will only strengthen the root of every fresh sorrow that takes hold of you. And to validate this fact, one need not look further than one's own life.

Thus, if you wish to oust sorrows and miseries from life, there is just one plain and simple solution - identify the root of the sorrow. And what is at the root of all your problems? Definitely, it is you yourself...! For, you have been accorded complete freedom by Nature, and therefore, you are yourself responsible for every sorrow plaguing you. And when you alone are to blame for your pitiable condition, then it is evident that the state you are in is the outcome of one of your own mistakes. And what is that mistake? The mistake is, trying to turn a blind eye to Nature's design. How so, you may ask? Well, in Nature's scheme of things, nothing save for your 'mind' belongs to you, but you still perpetually endeavour to make other people and objects your own. Now, regardless of your actions, nobody belongs to you, whether it is your house, car, business, friends or family. It is your delusion alone which prompts you to consider them as your own and prods you to create an illusory world as per your thinking. And this is where everything goes haywire. For, as per the ultimate design of Nature, even your body is not your own; it is but a medium to execute the tasks springing forth from the mind.

At this, you might counter, 'What is wrong in considering a few objects and people as our own?' Well, your naïve question makes it amply clear that presently, you have no conception of right and wrong. At present, you are completely in the grip of incorrect teachings, guided by your religion and community in your views of right and wrong. But none of them are the right measure to discern right from wrong; there is but one such perfect measure and that is Nature's design. Hence, if you live as per Nature's design, then you are on the right path; if not, then you are definitely treading the wrong path, and you will have to suffer sorrows and miseries as a consequence. Then, neither society nor religion will be able to deliver you from this suffering. Hence, if you wish to safeguard yourself from miseries and grief, you will simply have to honour Nature's design. Having said that, comprehend another design of Nature that will satiate all your queries; this design will elucidate the mistake you have been committing by considering people and objects as your own. It is the law of Nature that save for a human being's pure mind, everything in this world is both dynamic as well as changeable, and even your own body, which you consider your own, is no exception to this law. And when they are all subject to change, they will inevitably experience cycles of ups and downs. In other words, none of the objects or people that you consider your own can be shielded from hard times; besides, there is no way you can avert the hard times. And that is why, save for man's pure mind, everything here is unpredictable. At the same time, it is also true that apart from your mind, nothing here belongs to you. Perhaps now, you must have comprehended the root of your sorrows.

However, if you have failed to grasp this point yet, I shall explain it in greater detail. The cycle is set in motion when you begin to consider a few people and objects as your own, falling for fallacious beliefs, vain knowledge and the unnatural design drawn by the world. Whereas, the fact remains, they do not belong to you and neither can they ever do. Despite this, you establish a connection with them and end up violating Nature's ultimate design. Now, as per the principle of Nature, everything save for a human being's pure mind is subject to change in pace; hence, they all, including your own body, perpetually experience ups and downs. And as soon as they are caught in this vortex of ups and downs, sorrows and grief plague you. For example, no sooner your car breaks down than you become flustered; if your father becomes indisposed, you become grief-stricken and desolate. If you mull over this deeply, you will realise, there is but one common factor at the root of all these sorrows viz. you have established a connection with all these external objects by considering them your own. As a consequence, each blow rained upon them leaves you heartbroken, for then, every blow striking them is deemed by you as a blow to your own self. On the other hand, consider this scenario; you are unaffected when other people's cars meet with accidents or other people's parents succumb to illness. Because you have not established any connection of belongingness with them, and that absence of connection does not allow the wound to penetrate within. This verily proves the fact that desolation and grief prevail over you, only when the people, with whom you have established a connection of belongingness, get hurt. This begs the question, is there a concrete solution to free oneself from the shackles of woes and sorrows? Of course, there is! All you have to do is sever this connection of belongingness. You might try out a multitude of solutions, save for this, but you will always meet with failure. For, there is no solution except for following the principles of spiritual science.

Now, you might be tempted to counter, 'What will be left of our lives if we sever connections with others?' You are posing this question only because you find the very thought of severing the said connections to be impossible, as this is an age-old habit and you have been living with this mindset forever. Secondly, I am asking you to sever the connection, not to break your relations or bonds of affection; you can continue maintaining relations with everybody. In other words, you can enjoy your house, your car and the people in your life to the utmost and stand by them like a pillar of strength, lending a helping hand when any of them is burdened with difficulties. That is, indeed, your duty, but at the same time, you must also comprehend that this is the limit where you need to draw the line. If your father is ailing, then it is your duty to take him to the doctor, discharge the hospital bill and ensure that the best possible treatment is accorded to him. Indeed, you must ensure that you discharge all these duties, but then, stop right at this point. Do whatever is humanly possible for you to do, and then stop. Disconnect yourself from the upheavals that arise beyond this point; leave everything beyond this point to Nature's system of justice and the unpredictability of the world. Know that if you are unable to do this bit for yourself, then you will never find a release from the clutches of troubles and sorrows. Of course, the person who has imbibed step 1 properly will assuredly not find this arduous. Besides, just tell me, if you sever your connection with your car, will its ownership be claimed by someone else? If you stop considering it your own, will it stop lending you enjoyment? Absolutely not! Nothing of the sort will happen. On the contrary, when you adopt this stance, then whether it is a car or a person, you will derive even more enjoyment out of them, and most importantly, you will not wallow in misery and grief if some harm were to befall them. So, whether it is an object or a person, enjoy everyone's company to the hilt but your 'duty' should be the limit as far as your conduct is concerned. Accept once and for all that the other, whether it is an object or a person, is verily 'other'... Thus, save yourself from considering anybody else as your own. Enjoy that object or person for as long as you can, and when any harm befalls them, fulfil your duty towards them. Leave all the ups and downs beyond this point to Nature's system of justice. To state this point pithily, if you wish to cast away sorrows and miseries from your life, then you have no choice save for severing your connection with others. You might move heaven and earth, but if you do not put this solution to use, sorrows and miseries will continue to plague you forever. Moreover, the reason you are finding it a herculean task to actualise this is the conditioning you have been subjected to over the years; this habit has become so deeply embedded in you that it has become well-nigh difficult to break free of it. But you must decide once and for all that such a beautiful mind bestowed by Nature should assuredly not be allowed to suffer endlessly under the onslaught of sorrows and miseries. Trust me, this one staunch resolution on your part will make the way ahead much easier.

To drive home this point, I shall explain it with the example of Jesus Christ's life. As we all know, Jesus Christ dedicated his entire life in the service of ushering in a new dawn for humankind, but in what way did the world reciprocate his kindness? He was crucified, and countless nails were drilled into his body. However, this heinous act scarcely made a dent on Christ's pure mind. Do you know why? Because even as the nails were being driven into his body, Christ had severed his connection with his body long ago. Now, take a moment to ponder, despite the immeasurable physical agony, Christ could sever his connection with his body, so why can't you sever your connection with your house, car and relations? You most certainly can! And if you wish to dispel sorrows from your life, then you will indubitably have to do so. There is no recourse other than severing one's connection, in order to free oneself from the bondage of pains and sorrows.

Let me provide you a practical application that will ease the process. You might have heard of *Japa Mantra*, which means to continually repeat a single *mantra*. The '*Japa Mantra*' is verily the method for securing liberation from your sorrows. However, you must not start repeating nonsensical *mantras* culled out from the scriptures, like other people are wont to do, because that will not serve the purpose at all. Remember Krishna's teaching, 'Your life, your *mantra*'. In other words, even in the case of the *Japa Mantra*, you have no recourse but to become your own doctor; you have to write your own *Japa Mantra,* in your own words, to secure deliverance from sorrows and miseries. Ergo, without further ado, pen a few lines on the basis of whatever you have found significant from the points discussed in the preceding text. And then, I shall assist you in writing your first *mantra.* So, write, "I have comprehended that establishing a connection between my pure mind and the external world is verily the root cause of all my sorrows. And I simply do not want any trace of sorrow in my precious life. Ergo, I will derive enjoyment from everything, I will fulfil my duty towards everyone...but then, I will stop right there. I (hereby) sever my connection with every person and object that I consider my own." I have given you an allusion on how to write your *Japa Mantra*; now, take your time and write it down in your own words. And whenever you feel sorrow descending over you, contemplate over this *mantra* continually; get to the root of the sorrow tormenting you. By doing so, you will realise that there is no other reason at its root, save for considering something as your own. So, simply sever that attachment and you will promptly be liberated from the sorrow hounding you. This is your very own *Japa Mantra,* written by you in your own words and for yourself, so it is bound to be effective. You must comprehend that no other solution apart from this can help you oust the sorrows and miseries plaguing your life.

Your *Japa Mantra*

....

....

....

....

....

....

....

....

....

Having said that, it is not necessary for everything to fall into place in your very first attempt. For, not only is your habit of establishing connections a longstanding one, but your wounds are deep-seated too. But, in spite of this, you can effect quite a significant change immediately upon repeating the *Japa Mantra*, which you yourself have penned; to summarise, henceforth, whenever you find yourself plunging into despair, straightaway compose a *Japa Mantra* to vanquish that particular sorrow. To give an example, if your car has met with an accident and you find yourself spiralling into a sorrowful state, write a *Japa Mantra* at that very moment stating, 'The car has had an accident, not my mind. I am not going to take that car with me when I depart from this world, so why lament over it? I have now apprehended that I have got myself entrapped in this web of sorrow on account of considering that car to be my own. But it is not mine, is it? Besides, my car is not the only or the first vehicle to have met with an accident. Hundreds of thousands of car accidents occur every single day. So, I hereby sever my connection with my car...'

Similarly, widen your sphere, and henceforth, whenever you find yourself engulfed in any sorrow, compose a *Japa Mantra* for that sorrow; then sit calmly in solitude and repeat that *mantra* until the sorrow disappears or its grip on you weakens. This is the only effective solution to liberate yourself from woes and sorrows. If you embrace this solution, you will be delivered from any sorrow in a span of just a day or two, which otherwise would have plagued you for days and weeks on end. A day will soon dawn, when just like Christ, you will also succeed in severing all your connections with external objects. Indeed, you cannot even (begin to) imagine how utterly joyous life will become then. I can only show you the way and extend my best wishes to you. For the rest, you will have to conduct your own surgery in order to dispel sorrows and miseries from life, and I am certain you will do as much in order to lead a wonderful life.

B) Relieve Yourself of Tensions

There is no denying that every human being is beset with an endless spate of tensions weighing him down. A student is jittery about his performance in the examination, while a youth of marriageable age is apprehensive about finding a good life partner. If old age fills one with trepidation, another has misgivings about his health, while an undercurrent of tension continues to run through mutual relationships. In short, every human being, in lesser or greater degree, harbours stress and tension on multiple occasions. Having said that, sorrow, tension, fear, frustration and so on are mere synonyms in the lexicon of an ordinary human being. For, even today, the world is marked by a dearth of profound human psychology, and consequently, all of these negative emotions seem alike to scores of human beings. But they are gravely misunderstood; for, all negative emotions are unlike each other and there are distinct reasons behind the occurrence of each. But yes, all these negativities stem from the common root—establishing connectivity with the world without. That being said, tensions can be of multiple kinds, but on a fundamental basis, all tensions mask but one emotion—*what will the future hold?* To put it succinctly, whenever you establish a connection between your pure mind and your apprehension for the future, then regardless of the matter, you succumb to tension. Here, let me ask you, do you have any authority or control over what will transpire in the future? Are you certain of what will occur in the future or whether that eventuality will be in accordance with your wishes? In this world, even the trickling of a drop of water is the summation of millions of events; in that case, to worry oneself to naught in anticipation of a future event is, in itself, rank foolishness. But, despite this, everybody is wildly interested in 'what will happen'. And as long as you persist in establishing a connection with your fears for the future, tensions will continue to ensnare you, and no power on earth will be able to deliver you from such tensions. Pray tell me, had you wrested a guarantee from Nature on the eve of your birth that everything in your life will occur in accordance to your wishes? Had you been vested with some extraordinary power, thereby ensuring that everything should manifest in accordance to your will? And do you really think that everything will fall into place by fretting over what will happen? Before the battle of Mahabharata, Arjuna too was caught in the throes of worry and anxiety, fretting over, 'What will happen? Who will win?' And Krishna allayed his fears and asserted that this very thought is the seed that gives rise to tension. He averred, 'Fight, and fight with all your might and main, as you have never fought before, marshalling all your resources, and let the events thereafter run their own course.' I am also urging you to do the same; undertake your tasks to the best of your ability, and then let the future unfold in the manner it has to. Deal with it when it happens, why fret over it now? Similarly, in the life of a student, his aim should be to study with complete concentration and diligence, and not worry about the results. Besides, the majority of your 'worries about the future' are so ill-placed that they have absolutely no relation with your life. Countless times, you have harboured the tension of what an uncertain tomorrow will bring in its wake, but when the morrow arrives, you find that all your fears were unfounded; hence, why harbour unnecessary tension in the first place? Vest your trust in Nature's system of justice and leave your fears about the future at its doorstep. Continue to pursue your tasks with full diligence and fervour, and let the future unfold in the manner it deems fit.

Having guided you this far, let me now show you a simple and effective method to shield yourself from tension. All you must do is think about the present moment and present day, that is all! Endeavour to do your best today, in whichever sphere of life you can; do not think of anything above and beyond it. This one change will dispel all your 'worries of the future'. Comprehend once and for all that there is no other reason at the root of your tensions other than establishing a connection between your pure mind and your apprehension about the future. In other words, tensions will continue dogging your footsteps unless you sever this connection. Let me cite the example of Buddha to elucidate this statement. As you may well know, Buddha was born in an era when Hinduism was the only religion followed in India. However, the prevalent norms, traditions and hypocritical rituals of Hinduism went against the very grain of Buddha's belief; ergo, he raised his voice and began to vehemently oppose the shams of Hinduism. Unfazed and fearless, he did not stop to think, 'What will happen if I take such a step?' 'How will the fanatic Hindus and their *pundits* react, and what action will they take?' 'Oh, let them do what they want; let what has to happen, happen,' Buddha thought, for, all he was concerned with was the course of action to be taken; the aftermath of his actions and the reaction of others did not matter to him in the least. Vociferous in his protest against the hypocrisies of Hinduism that lasted for almost 35 years, he eventually went on to establish a new religion called Buddhism. Consequently, Buddha became a great personality; a man whom the entire world reveres today. Now, pause and reflect, what would have happened had he thought even once about what will transpire in the future? He would have simply not been able to attain the stature of an enlightened personality and become the great Buddha as we know him. Had he given in to his fears, he would have found himself incapable of speaking against the hypocrisies of Hinduism. Surmise from this example, how dangerous and detrimental all your fears pertaining to the future really are! Just think about the humungous amount of stress and pressure you are subjected to on their account. In fact, it is these very fears that do not let you perform with determination and perseverance.

Ergo, one simply must rid oneself of tension, because to spend the beautiful life granted by Nature in the durance vile of anxiety and tension is a disgrace to human life. And the root of all tensions is nothing but establishing a connection with fear regarding the future. So, firmly sever your connection with all 'worries of the future' and set yourself free from all kinds of tension. And for that purpose, seek the help of your *Japa Mantra* once again. Resolve that from this day onwards, 'I will simply not think about what the future has in store for me. If I am feeling stressed, then it is verily my own fault. No sooner do I lead my thoughts on the rickety pathways of uncertainty about the future than my mind is submerged in tension. In other words, I myself dump the onerous burden of grief and tension on my shoulders.' Remember what Krishna had proclaimed; a human being is his own friend and enemy. 'Thus, from today onwards, I will stop thinking about what the future will hold. I will simply not step beyond what is required of me today.' Write a *Japa Mantra* around these lines and perform a precise surgery over your thoughts in your own words. Whenever you find yourself becoming stressed and anxiety-ridden, repeat the *Japa Mantra* written by yourself, and your tension will soon be swept away. Remember, you are writing your own scripture, a scripture so great that it will guide you all your life.

Your *Japa Mantra*

....

....

....

....

....

....

....

....

....

Thus, whenever you find any tension surge within you like a gigantic wave, threatening to submerge you, repeat this *Japa Mantra* composed by yourself and the tension gripping you will weaken and vanish. Whenever you feel stressed, get to its root and you will find that, in the end, you are yourself to blame for it and that it is directly connected with your fear for the future. So, from today onwards, whenever tension seizes hold of you, get to its root and write a new *Japa Mantra* for it. Once composed, sit in solitude and repeat the *Japa Mantra* of your own making till the time that tension disappears. For, such a beautiful life cannot be squandered in harbouring the tension of what tomorrow will bring; it can best be lived with a lion-hearted approach of facing whatever the future unfolds with a smile on one's face. And if you wish to live with such intrepidity, then you will simply have to sever your connections with all vexing thoughts of anticipation regarding your future. We are discussing the ultimate truth of spiritual science in the scientific age and learning to live our lives as per Nature's design. Nature has prevailed since millions of billions of years and its design and principles have been in existence ever since. Thus, if not me, then at least honour the design of Nature. Kindly do not seek the refuge of religious communities in order to oust your worries, else you will contract yet another fear of whether you will attain heaven or languish in hell, or whether you will attain *moksha* (salvation). Hence, know this for certain, if you wish to be freed of all tensions, you will have to sever your connection with all thoughts on the lines of what the future will bring. And I am confident that you will do so with the assistance of your *Japa Mantra*. Furthermore, I am also sanguine that henceforth, you will sever your connection with all kinds of futile, fantastical pronouncements, and at once, accept the refuge of Nature's ultimate design.

C) Safeguard Yourself from Becoming Upset

In this world of ours, becoming upset, that is to say, taking offence and nursing a wounded heart is the principal problem faced by people. And when the mind is upset, one becomes good for nothing, a bumbling mass at best; neither one's wealth nor family, neither religion nor society prove to be of any use. Well, what we must ask ourselves is, why do we get hurt time and again? When posed with this question, every person will think up some reason or the other, essentially holding others culpable for their wounded feelings. And, herein lies the folly, for, as I have stated earlier, a human being is completely free. Ergo, he simply cannot lay the blame on others for his heartache and wounded feelings. Therefore, it is you who must find the reason that drove you to commit the mistake and has led you to this abject state; the fact is, you alone are at fault, so try to get to the root of your heartache. And I have reiterated time and again that there is just one thing at the root of all your negative emotions, and that is, establishing a connection with the external world. So, whenever you get hurt or become upset, keenly observe what lies at its root. You will find that you have established a connection with the external world on account of some expectation, and in turn, that connection has emerged as the reason for you being upset and hurt.

Indeed, harbouring expectations is, in itself, a queer kind of lunacy, regardless of whether you harbour those expectations from people or objects. Nobody will act in accordance with your wishes, as you are not their master. Despite this, a human being harbours expectations, especially from fellow human beings. Why do you think this is the case? There is but one reason for this; whenever anyone in this world does anything for another person, he feels that he is doing the other person a favour. And when he considers himself bestowing a favour, then in return, he expects the other person to behave in a particular way. Owing to his expectations, he then inadvertently establishes a connection with that person's future behaviour. But he fails to realise that the other person is also completely free; he is at liberty to do whatever he wishes, at any given point of time. That is precisely why, all kinds of expectations are fundamentally wrong, and if truth be told, these expectations are the greatest impediment to a human being's relationships. For, you harbour expectations from other people and they fall short of your expectations...and consequently, your heart gets wounded. Likewise, the other person has also harboured some expectations from you and his feelings are hurt when you do not meet them. Consequently, this vicious cycle repeats itself with regularity, and people continue to hurt each other, day in and day out, as a result of which a huge chasm develops in relationships. I hope you must have now comprehended, why your feelings have become so fragile that they get hurt at the slightest instance, and you must have also apprehended the reason for the bitterness simmering in your relationships. You must have also discerned that expectations are akin to a poison that is slowly gnawing away at your life. After having discussed the previous points at length, I believe you must have now become well-acquainted both with human mind and Nature's design, and I can now proceed with explaining matters in brief.

So far, you must have surely grasped the fact that 'expectations' are at the root of all the occurrences, wherein one's feelings get wounded. So, without further ado, let me throw light on how you can liberate yourself from expectations, for, until you do so, you will continue to experience heartache, on account of people, objects and circumstances. Ergo, the simple solution to steer clear of expectations is, do good unto others only till the point where no expectations are arising within you, on account of the beneficence you are casting on them. Engage in helping others only to the extent that no expectations are surfacing within you. If expectations are surging within you upon doing something for a person, then simply stay your hand...and stop yourself. Otherwise, you will only lay down the foundation for future heartache and distress. For, it is certain that the other person will fall short of meeting your expectations, but even so, this is a mistake which every human being perpetually repeats. Parents tend to their children and go the extra mile to do many things for them, and then, they inadvertently harbour expectations from them. Now, nobody in this world can meet the expectations of others for the simple reason that expectations are a figment of your imagination, while the other person's freedom is his reality. This game of chasing expectations is constantly being played out everywhere, between spouses, family, friends, colleagues, and so on. Everyone bends backwards to help others but not without harbouring expectations from them. Consequently, everybody's feelings are battered, day in and day out, which in turn sows the seeds of acrimony in relationships. Although, this does not mean that you should stop doing good turns towards others; you must certainly lend a helping hand as far as possible, but when expectations take a firm grip over you, stop in your tracks immediately and limit your actions. Do a good turn unto others only to the extent that it does not beget expectations in you.

In short, if you value your peace of mind, and want to save yourself from getting upset, throttle the very expectations that arise within you. You have no recourse but to do so, because nobody in this world is ever going to meet other people's expectations. Let me elucidate this by citing the example of God himself. Every human being cherishes countless expectations from God. Now, take a look at your life and tell me, how many expectations of yours are being fulfilled? Just reflect, when even the Almighty God is falling short of your expectations, how can a fellow human being ever meet your expectations? In the same vein, let us take the example of the Bhagavad Gita. Krishna was expounding the ultimate truth of Nature to Arjuna, and what Krishna was expounding was indubitably in Arjuna's best interests. But Arjuna was busy brandishing his own knowledge and invoking the so-called knowledge of religion and the scriptures. He kept putting forward one argument after another to supplement his decision to not fight the war. Even so, Krishna did not let Arjuna's behaviour upset him; instead, he persevered in his exposition to Arjuna till it stretched to eighteen long chapters! How did he do so...? Krishna managed to pull off this incredible feat simply because he harboured no expectations from Arjuna. Pray tell, what would have happened had he nursed the expectation, "Arjuna should immediately grasp what a person like me, a man of such great stature, is explaining to him." Or that, "Arjuna should simply not reason with an *antaryami* like me, a person who is highly conversant with the matters of the mind." Can you guess what would have happened then? Krishna's feelings would have been hurt; he would have become upset. And in this irked state of mind, he wouldn't have been able to sustain his explanations to Arjuna till eighteen chapters. He would have declared halfway through the Gita, "Arjuna, do as you please and get lost!" That is why, Krishna says, "I am entitled only to the action, not to its fruit." Krishna concerns himself with the deed of explaining to Arjuna, but he does not expect cooperation from Arjuna as an outcome of his deed. He does not wish for any fruit, in the form of respect from Arjuna, in return. And let me state with authority that you shall not be liberated from the shackles of your heartaches and distress as long as you do not become like Krishna. Do for others and do as much as you can, but hold no expectations in return, for, no sooner you harbour expectations than your feelings will get hurt. Agreed, you cannot transform your thought process and become like Krishna in just one day, and that is perfectly fine, but stop doing for others from the very moment you find expectations rearing their ugly head. The moment the seed of expectations is sown and begins to sprout, pull back immediately and limit your actions. Kindly do this small favour unto yourself, if only to save yourself.

To state briefly, do not establish a connection with other people's behaviour by way of expectations. Simply embrace this habit and attain deliverance from getting hurt for good. In order to effect this change within yourself, take the assistance of the *Japa Mantra* once again. Write in your own words, "I wish to be liberated from getting my feelings wounded for good. Beyond a doubt, all kinds of expectations are at the root of heartache. Thus, from this day onwards, I will not nurse expectations for whenever I do anything for anyone. I will not let myself be ruffled and disturbed if the receiver does not reciprocate in a desirable manner. And the moment I feel expectations rearing their head, I will restrain my actions and withdraw myself from doing anything more for that person." Write this down in your own words and conceive a *Japa Mantra* for yourself. At every available opportunity, repeat this *mantra*; the repeated affirmations will steadily weaken your habit of nursing expectations, and eventually, a day will dawn when you will no longer fall prey to heartache or disappointment. Besides, this is the sole solution that will bring you deliverance from heartache, for, you are completely aware of how disturbed and agitated you feel when your feelings are hurt. In your disturbed state of mind, you are reduced to a good-for-nothing, incapable of carrying out even your daily activities. So, in order to make your life glorious and beautiful, liberate yourself from being upset and agitated for good.

Your *Japa Mantra*

....

....

....

....

....

....

....

....

....

Perhaps, everything will not be set right at once with this one step, but that is perfectly fine. Simply incorporate this *Japa Mantra* composed by yourself as an integral part of your life, and henceforth, whenever you find yourself getting disturbed, dig down to its root and ascertain its connection with expectations. And then, compose a fresh *Japa Mantra* concurrently, as per the prevalent situation, and keep repeating it till the time you are liberated from heartache. If you wish to be joyous in life, firmly abide by the decision that you shall not live with negative emotions. All you have to do is make a firm resolve;

besides, I am always here to support and aid you, providing you with the best possible solution. Ergo, grab this opportunity that has come your way and utilise it to the optimum.

D) Overcome Your Fears

Indeed, apprehension and fear are the biggest impediments to living a beautiful life. Man, on a daily basis, contracts ever-new fears, and every fear he contracts entirely spirits away his zest for life. If truth be told, living in perpetual fear is akin to dying, because a terrified person is nothing more than a breathing corpse, one who can neither laugh heartily nor revel in joy or live a carefree life. Furthermore, he becomes incapable of performing tasks effectively. This raises the moot question, why is man beset with fears? Well, having progressed this far with our discussion, I see scant need to elucidate any further on the reason behind this; the gist is, you are yourself responsible for every mental suffering that is plaguing you. Thus, you have no other recourse but to apprehend your own fault with regard to every mental suffering you are tormented with. And by now, you must have also comprehended that the root cause of all your suffering is, establishing a connection with the external world. In this regard, let us now comprehend the spiritual science of fear. Frankly speaking, I fail to comprehend why man disregards Nature's design, and why he displays such stark ineptitude in comprehending that nothing in this world belongs to him, except for his pure mind. Despite knowing this fact, every human being commits the mistake of considering a multitude of objects and people as his own. And then he suffers, as he does not wish to lose that which he considers his own. Observe keenly from this day onwards; you will find that it is the fear of losing someone or something which lies at the root of all your fears. Now, the moot question to ask is, is the world functioning as per the wishes of human beings? No, it certainly is not! It is functioning only as per the ultimate laws established by Nature, which state that nothing belongs to man, except for his own pure mind. Whether it is objects or people, he has to invariably part from them, if not today then tomorrow, and eventually, one day, he himself has to depart from this world, leaving all his possessions and relations behind. This being the case, why dwell upon when and what object or person would part from you? Why fritter away your energy worrying about parting from someone or become anxious over someone being upset with you? This certainly won't do! You will simply have to put a rein on all such thoughts, because no sooner you entertain such notions than you are bound to be caught in the grip of fear. And what is man's greatest fear? The fear of death, of course. This leads us to the next obvious question, why does man contract the fear of death? Man contracts this fear, because he starts considering his body as his own, and he does so to such an extent that he simply does not wish to be parted from it. But regardless of the body and the person inhabiting that body, it verily has to part with the pure mind one day; even great men such as Buddha, Christ and Krishna were not an exception to this law. But even so, owing to the fallacy of considering the body as being one's own, the fear of death plagues one and all. Even Arjuna had contracted the same fear in the battle of Mahabharata, whereby he was haunted by the thought, 'What if I get killed in this war?' But to rid him of his fear, Krishna had explained to Arjuna at the time that, 'You are separate and distinct from your body; thus, neither should you worry about your own body nor other people's bodies.'

With this elucidation, you must have comprehended the entire spiritual science behind fear. And if you have still not gained absolute clarity, I will lend you a little more assistance. Stated in simple terms, considering other people and objects as your own is at the root of all your fears; basically, it is establishing the connection that 'This is mine.' And once you have established such a connection, an unknown fear—the fear of loss—holds you in its vice-like grip. You simply fail to realise that your body, in actuality, does not belong to you. Ergo, unless you sever the connection of 'belongingness', you will perpetually be plagued by the fear of losing and parting from people and objects. There is no other way to untangle the complex knot of fear and be free of it; neither did such a possibility exist in the past, nor is it likely to exist in the present or the future. And if you wish for happiness and peace to suffuse this precious life you have been bestowed with, then you simply have no option but to sever this connection. Else, you will set off on all sorts of absurd paths in order to dispel your fears; you will continue seeking assurances in a multitude of places and live an inconsequential life, placing your faith in myriad nonsensical teachings. In fact, the greater majority of people are already hopelessly mired in entanglements, paying heed to absurd declarations. Nevertheless, know this for certain, instead of abating, you will only experience a surge in your fears with such pointless endeavours. You can be liberated from fear only through spiritual science, and as far as that solution is concerned, it is simple and straightforward. Whether it is an object or a person, sever all your connections of belongingness with them. Having said that, I am sure you will initially find this task challenging, because old habits die hard; besides, you have been waylaid and have fallen prey to wrong instructions since a very long time. But even so, one has to find a solution to eradicate fear.

Hence, to liberate yourself from your fears, accept the refuge of the *Japa Mantra* once again. Compose your own *Japa Mantra* and write, 'I own nobody, except for my pure mind. Everyone else comes into my life only to part from me eventually. The only question which remains is, whether they will part from me now or in the future. So, they can part from me whenever they want; that decision lies with the one who will part from me and the very design of Nature. Why should I live in fear by unnecessarily dwelling upon it? Everyone is free to part from me whenever they want and get upset with me whenever they wish. But I will enjoy each moment with every person and object for the duration they are with me. Else, whatever happens with any person or object and whenever it occurs is verily not in my hands, because that power is completely vested in Nature's system of justice.' Compose a *Japa Mantra* of your own in this manner and whenever you get the chance, ponder over it and repeat it in solitude. And whenever fear overcomes you, begin to recite the *mantra* immediately. With this exercise, not only will your fears abate, but one day they will also be dispelled forever.

....

....

....

....

....

E) Cast Out Insecurity

Insecurity is a grave problem plaguing mankind, and a person gripped by insecurity becomes incapable of performing any task effectively. This is a negative emotion which devours a person from within, and it is needless to reiterate here that nobody other than you is at fault for your insecurities as well. And do you know where your fault lies? Irrefutably, the fault lies in your dependency. Regardless of the kind of dependency it is, whether financial, mental, emotional or social, no sooner you become dependent on a person than you start becoming insecure about that person. In simple words, you establish a connection of your dependency with a particular person, and then, as a consequence, you have to live your life being tormented by a deadly feeling called insecurity. And this, indeed, is deplorable! Man, who was bestowed with the stature of a king by Nature, has been reduced to live lifelessly, gripped by negative emotions at all times.

Now, having stated this, I am assured that you have become discerning enough to have fathomed its remedy. Yes, you are right! Complete independence is the only solution to this problem. In other words, severing connections of dependencies with others, of every manner and kind, is the only solution to this problem. And unless you successfully sever all such connections, you will continue to be insecure; bear in mind that nothing else can deliver you from the clutches of insecurity. And, if a person himself is not self-dependent, then neither Nature nor I can be held accountable for it. I am elucidating the spiritual science of the design fabricated by Nature to you. I am making your path easier by trying to liberate you from the shackles of delusions and aimless wandering. I state plainly and clearly that you will not be able to cast out insecurity unless you relinquish all kinds of dependencies. Ergo, derive the utmost enjoyment from everything and everybody in your life, but do not become wholly dependent upon anyone. To state this in Krishna's parlance, the other person is nothing but a medium, be it for your joy or sorrow, and it is you who have to live your life standing on your own two feet. So, do not tarry, for, it is not too late even now. Seize as much enjoyment as you can from everything, whether it is an object, person or pursuit, but do not dwell upon it too much. If, in the future, that person or the situation changes, let it change, and be prepared to adjust and adapt yourself to the changed situation. For, you cannot claim ownership of the other person, and accordingly, he is not bound to live his life in accordance to your wishes either. Why then do you become increasingly reliant on that person? The truth of the matter is, you wish to wield the whip and become the master of everything under the sun, but caught in that delusion, you ironically become the slave of that very thing. Now, tell me, when you are not even your own master, how can you become anybody else's master? Dependency implies that you wish to own something at any cost, and when you want something regardless of the consequences, you are enslaved by the very desire of owning that thing. Indeed, when you cannot live without something, you are as good as a slave. Besides, your dependency is not limited to people; you are a slave to everything, whether it is wealth or other material possessions. Ironically, you misapprehend yourself as the master, whereas, in fact, you are nothing but a slave. Let me narrate the tale of a Sufi *fakir* to further shed light on this point. Once there lived a Sufi *fakir* who would pose a question to anybody he encountered on his way, and if he found anything wanting in their answer, he would straightaway explain the truth to them in his own inimitable style. One day, while he was out on a stroll, he espied a washerman leading his donkey with a rope tied to the creature's neck. He immediately sprinted up to him and asked, "Sir, can you help me out?"

"Certainly!" replied the washerman.

The *fakir* observed, "Actually, I am a little confused. I see both you and the donkey tied by the same rope, so I cannot fathom, who amongst you is the master? Is it you or the donkey?"

The washerman looked at the *fakir* in disbelief on being asked such a preposterous question, wondering if he was a madman roaming around in the guise of a *fakir*, but then he shrugged his shoulders and thought that he might as well answer his question. Thinking thus, he responded, "Why, you cannot even comprehend something so elementary? I am the master, of course! Can't you see that there is a rope tied around the donkey's neck, and I am leading the animal, holding the rope's end?"

Hearing this, the *fakir* peered closely, first at the washerman, and then at the donkey. Then, suddenly, struck by some notion, he cut the rope from the middle. No sooner was the rope cut than the donkey fled, and seeing his animal running off, the washerman also sped off in its pursuit. Seeing the washerman run, the *fakir* bellowed after him, "See, you were wrong! The donkey is the master, not you. That is why you are running after it."

Your condition is no different from that of the washerman. You have let innumerable donkeys hold sway over you, allowing them to become your masters, and there are countless people you are dependent on in order to live your life. Such being the way of things, insecurity is bound to creep into every small occurrence in your life. But there is one solution that can help you safeguard yourself from this. Accept the refuge of the *Japa Mantra* once again and start severing all your dependencies with its aid. Write in your *Japa Mantra*, 'Why should I be dependent on others despite being born as a human being? Everyone is free to be a part of my life, as long as they wish to. Others can shower their largesse on me if they wish to, and likewise, they are free to stop too. I am not dependent upon anybody, am I? I know I am fully capable of living my life in my own way. And besides, why should I nurse a terrible emotion like insecurity today, in the fear that somebody's behaviour would change towards me or they would part from me in the future? Why should I not simply become my own master? Why should I give others the power to reduce my life to shambles by being dependent on them?' So, compose a *Japa Mantra* for yourself along these lines, and whenever you find yourself caught in the grip of insecurity, sit in solitude and repeat this *Japa Mantra* continually. And from today itself, severe all your insecurities one by one and become as self-reliant as possible. For that matter, the person you are dependent on is bound to repress you, for, you have given him the key to your happiness. If truth be told, this is not how life should be lived. But alas, everyone is caught in the throes of helplessness. Go and ask your religion, society and family as to why you are not self-reliant, or better still, pose this question to your education system. What is it that they have taught and expounded to you that you have been reduced to this state of dependency on others with regard to everything? And especially where women are concerned, religion and society have left no stone unturned to suppress and subjugate them. They have been beaten and battered into such dependency that they have been rendered incapable of taking even one breath of freedom and security; living in constant fear and dread, they have become utterly helpless and powerless.

Well, I have done my bit by endeavouring to explain the remedy for obliterating insecurity, basing all my explanations on the premise of spiritual science. Now, it is up to you to write your *Japa Mantra* in your own words and contemplate over it continually. So, without further ado, reduce dependency and increase self-reliance with its aid; and remember, there is no other way to dispel insecurity.

Your *Japa Mantra*

....

....

....

....

F) Break Free from Frustration

Frustration is a peculiar kind of negative emotion; it generally grips a person when he does not live up to his own expectations. In other words, when a human being raises his expectations from himself and is unable to meet them, he finds himself in the grip of frustration. This implies, harbouring expectations from oneself has a direct connection with frustration. Having stated this, there is no harm in a human being nursing expectations from himself. The moot question, however, is, why is a human being not able to meet his expectations? Does he lack talent and potential? No, definitely not! Both of these exist in every human being to some extent or the other, but oft-times, man is unable to perform as per his potential. His energy fails him, and the sole reason for this is, all other negative emotions devour every ounce of his life energy. So, if you wish to live up to your expectations, then you must break free from the shackles of all negative emotions; only then will you be able to fulfil your expectations, and then alone will you be able to get rid of frustration. Although, there are many people who also become frustrated when undesirable occurrences continually befall their lives. In other words, such people are inexorably entrapped in a vortex, by establishing a connection between the events that transpire and their expectations of how those events should have transpired. But, fortunately, all such frustrations have a short gestation period, hence they do not last for long. To state pithily, any kind of frustration invariably has a direct correlation with the self. However, these frustrations are no grave matter, for, man quickly recovers from them. Even so, if you wish to safeguard yourself from the onslaught of frustrations, indulge in any of your interests fully and unreservedly at least once during the day. Doing so, you will not be gripped by frustration even when you fall short of your expectations; and here, I need to emphasise that there is nothing wrong in holding expectations from oneself. In fact, even those who have attained greatness fall short of meeting their expectations numerous times. Now, if you wish to scale the pinnacle of greatness, it is imperative to harbour certain expectations from yourself. In such instances, oftentimes, a person is not able to fulfil his expectations, but this is not inherently wrong. Because many frustrations of this kind usher in a positive outcome as well, and propel a human being on the path of progress.

Having said that, there is yet another kind of frustration and an extremely dangerous one to boot. And that is the frustration resulting out of the suppression of a deeply-held and intense wish; a frustration of this kind can torment you all through your life. The perils of harbouring this kind of frustration are extremely debilitating, and more often than not, it becomes a herculean task to dispel its ominous shadow from one's life. I am certain, you must have encountered such frustrated people, who keep venting their frustration and entering into altercations with others, with or without reason. Ergo, it is necessary to exercise caution so as to not contract this kind of frustration, and you need to make only one resolution in order to do so, viz. never suppress your innermost desires under any circumstances. Then, pay no mind if someone is chiding you for harbouring such a desire or is acting as an impediment to you fulfilling it. For, they have nothing to lose, but it may prove costly to you, because your frustration will amplify and hound you till your last breath. In short, come what may, never suppress and kill your innermost desires, else be certain that you will be ruined. Ergo, pass a firm resolution so that you never contract frustrations of any sort. At this juncture, it is needless to explain how to compose your *Japa Mantra* for this purpose. But let me give you one final piece of advice. If you happen to encounter an exceedingly frustrated person, who is suppressing some deep desire, do not lock horns with him. Turn a blind eye to him and cut him off from your life, otherwise such a frustrated person will sap you of all your life energy.

Your *Japa Mantra*

....

....

....

....

....

....

....

G) Keep Depression at Bay

Depression is a newly-coined, modern mental ailment that is a topic of great discussion nowadays. But what is depression, after all? Depression implies feeling aimless and rudderless within one's own self. To find life meaningless and purposeless can also be termed as depression. And whoever is plagued by depression is wracked by low, debilitating feelings emerging from deep within himself. Now, what could be the reason behind this? Well, simply comprehend that just like frustration, depression is also an illness spawned out of establishing a faulty connection with oneself. Simply stated, if a human being repeatedly establishes a connection between himself and boredom, he becomes the most likely victim of depression and eventually succumbs to it one day. Likewise, there is also a distinct possibility that a person who constantly leads a mechanical life will someday fall prey to depression. Now, the initial stage of any kind of depression is unhappiness; ergo, if you find yourself turning morose all of a sudden, without reason, beware! Else, one day, this sadness will drag you into the pits of depression and scrambling out of it will be a herculean task. This begs the question, how can you safeguard yourself from depression? Simply by ensuring that you do not continually establish your connection with boredom and ennui; at the same time, safeguard yourself from leading a mechanical life at all times. Infuse a little vibrancy into your routine by taking time out to engage in activities that interest you; indulge in your hobbies with passion whenever you find a chance. Upon doing so, you will never find yourself in the doldrums. Also, whenever dark, grim thoughts grip you and you start feeling low-spirited for no conceivable reason, be cautious and immediately start seeking ways to make yourself happy and merry once again. Ensure that the misery pulling you down does not metamorphose into depression and if by some mischance, you do get depressed and dispirited, do not make haste and conclude that it is a mental illness. Else, you will be inexorably sucked into the trap of medicines and the malady will imprison you in its confines for a long time. Simply explain to yourself that it is the consequence of a monotonous life and constant boredom; that it is the consequence of living a superficial life, devoid of love. And, once you have grasped this notion, immediately start indulging in pursuits that bring you joy and pleasure; satiate your gastronomical urges with the food you love, wear what you like and pander to all your other interests as well. Spend quality time with the people you love and revel in their company. In the beginning, all these pursuits may not really hold your attention and you may do them listlessly, half-heartedly, but with persistence and dogged determination, the veils of darkness gripping your heart will lift and everything will be right with your inner world. The sooner you become immersed in your hobbies, the faster your depression will dissipate into thin air!

The above-mentioned scenario is just one aspect of falling prey to depression. Let me cite another reason for people sinking deep into depression. If your life revolves around a single person, then needless to say, trouble is bound to be your lot. For, if that person were to deceive you or is parted from you for some reason, you will succumb to depression. And this kind of depression will hold you in its grip for months and years together. Thus, do not let your life revolve around a single person, as doing so can prove to be fatal at any time. For, in such a case, your very dependency on that person will shatter you and ruin your life. Besides, you are a human being, so as far as possible, live your life under your own steam; this one remedy can act as an elixir to chase away many problems of life.

Therefore, make a firm resolve that you will not let depression creep within, and compose a *Japa Mantra* for yourself for that purpose. I am sure that henceforth, you do not require assistance to draft your *Japa Mantra*. Ergo, whenever you find yourself feeling low and morose, go on repeating the *Japa Mantra* written by you, and your unhappiness will never assume the monstrous form of depression.

....

....

....

....

....

....

....

H) Steer Clear of Disappointment and Despondency

Disappointment and despondency are also strange feelings which often swiftly swoop down on those who nurse great desires and lofty ambitions. For, as a rule, such people arrive at a wrong estimation of their capability, and furthermore, as their mind remains entangled in lofty desires, they are not even able to put in a good performance. And always remember, it is superlative performance which brings positive outcomes. Consequently, the day dawns when such people start believing that they are a failure, and that they have been defeated in the race of life. These are the very people who eventually succumb to disappointment and despondency. Therefore, everyone needs to comprehend that mere wishes do not lead to outcomes; ambitions do not turn into reality just by cherishing them lovingly; it is only superlative performance that brings results in life. Desires and ambitions, on the contrary, act as barriers to performance, and one cannot hope to achieve success without performance. Thus, consider desires and ambitions as nothing but your enemies. Ask yourself, although everybody nurtures wishes to attain a great number of things, do all those wishes translate into reality? No, they certainly don't! So, be wise; instead of chasing desires and ambitions, channelise your life energy into performance. If you perform well consistently, you are bound to progress and furthermore, upon doing so, you will safeguard yourself from falling prey to disappointment and despondency. This is verily the principle of life. Else, life will not transpire in sync with your desires, and consequently, you will be gripped by despondency and disappointment. This was verily the reason why Krishna emphasised the importance of forsaking the expectation of the fruits of one's actions. A sensible person that you are, you must have comprehended the spiritual science of despondency and despair, and I hope, you will now pen your own *Japa Mantra* and reap its benefit. I am confident that from now onwards, you will disengage your focus from desires and aim it onto performance.

Your *Japa Mantra*

....

....

....

....

....

....

....

I) Protect Yourself from Physical Maladies

We are all cognisant of the importance of our physical self, and therefore, we all wish to keep ourselves physically healthy. For this purpose, a myriad of edicts dealing with human health are commonplace in the world, and science has also made great strides to ensure the well-being of the human body. Notwithstanding this, man continues to succumb to one or the other ailment. Therefore, let us comprehend a few key points with respect to the human body. Firstly, everything alluded in relation to the body is based on possibilities; that is to say, nothing is exact and precise. Now, I can speak about the negativities of the mind with certainty, but I cannot speak with the same assurance and authority regarding the human body. For, the mind has a science of its own based on Nature's laws, but the body has always been unpredictable. As a rule, it is said that consuming tobacco causes cancer, but there are millions of people who do not fall prey to oral cancer, despite regularly consuming tobacco. The contrary stands true too, for, there are millions who have fallen prey to oral cancer without ever having partaken of tobacco. The same phenomenon can be seen not only with respect to food but also in the case of people consuming all kinds of drugs. There are many who subsist on soup, salad and fruits and yet fall sick, while those who devour huge quantities of fattening food live longer lives, bursting with health and vitality. Simply stated, even science can provide no accurate answer regarding the illness a human being might contract at any given time or even the manner in which he may contract the illness. This, however, does not imply that there has been no advancement in the field of medical science; indeed, science has assuredly performed one marvellous feat after another. And I hold it in highest esteem for this very reason; if life is beautiful today, then medical science has a major role to play in it. Nevertheless, all I wish to emphasise is, even today, we have scarce knowledge when it comes to the workings of the human body. Furthermore, you must also apprehend that mankind might never garner a complete understanding of the human body. For, the body will continue to confound human beings and it will forever play new tricks on us. A critically ill person might live for a few more decades, while a hale and hearty person might drop dead in an instant, and all such shenanigans will continue to transpire till eternity. A person with high cholesterol levels might live a healthy life without ever suffering a heart attack, while on the other hand, a person with healthy cholesterol levels might die in his prime due to heart failure. Indeed, this is a common occurrence that we have all witnessed, one which we have seen transpiring time and again.

This brings us to the question, why is this so? Well, the answer lies in Nature's design, wherein only the pure mind is predictable, whereas man's body and intelligence are unpredictable by their very nature. Thus, one can easily predict what people like Krishna and

Buddha, who lived with a pure mind, would do, because owing to its stability, a pure mind is predictable. But to divine what a person driven by his intelligence and ego will do at any moment is next to impossible. That is why, you always err in predicting how a person will behave at any moment; more often than not, he will act in stark contrast to what you had thought he would do. In short, you must comprehend that while the teachings laid out by the community and society at large might have some grain of truth in them, the ultimate truth is verily Nature's design. Likewise, science's knowledge and discoveries are vital too, but they too lie within the confines of Nature's design. And as the body is unpredictable as per Nature's design, it is well-nigh impossible to make any definitive claim with regard to it. And this is the very point I am trying to elucidate.

Now that we have comprehended the workings of the human body, the next logical question which follows is, how can one keep one's physique in good health? So, firstly, examine your body in juxtaposition with the various possibilities that have been laid out by science concerning the human body. As a first step, comprehend the tendency of your body; in this case too, you must become your own doctor, as all human bodies are essentially different. Simply stated, it is quite possible that what may work for one body may not work for another. Besides, your body invariably gives you indications about everything, by intimating you of what doesn't agree with it; so, even the simple act of choosing the food you consume should be based on whether it agrees with your body's constitution. If you find yourself struggling to digest fattening food or certain cuisines, then do not partake of such food which does not suit your constitution. Likewise, take into account the prevailing observations of science as well. Even though the blood report designed by science may not be perfect, it is quite precise from the point of view of possibilities. So, you must respect every parameter of science, and I am confident that you will certainly do this much for the sake of your physical health.

But having stated this, you must also comprehend that not everything will fall into place by putting this into practice; you will simply have to become your own doctor in the strictest sense, in order to derive maximum benefit and better possibilities for your health. For, in Nature's design, you are your best doctor and by now, you must have also apprehended this fact. In the same vein, comprehend another point with respect to Nature's design; in Nature's scheme of things, time influences your space and likewise, space invariably influences your time. In other words, your mind perpetually influences your body and vice versa. When you suffer from a headache, your mind indubitably becomes morose, whereas when your mind is jubilant, it assuredly helps you endure a stomach ache with ease. In short, as per Nature's design, the mind and body persistently influence each other wholly and absolutely. Now, everybody is extremely diligent in taking care of their physical well-being in order to maintain optimum health, but despite employing all possible means, where is it that you or science are faltering? Well, you falter when you turn a blind eye to the influence your mind casts over your body, when in fact, your 'time' i.e. your mind is far more powerful than your 'space' i.e. your body. In other words, the influence of your mind on your body is far more profound, and all the negative emotions which we have discussed so far are mental maladies that wreak havoc on your body. The truth is, the psychological reasons behind a human being succumbing to various ailments are far more culpable than physical ones. To give an example, if an illness strikes both, a person with a happy mindset and someone with a miserable mindset, the former will soon shake off the illness, while the latter might just succumb to that illness. In short, all I want you to comprehend is, if you wish to maintain your physical health, then it is imperative to shield your mind from all negativities, for, every form of negativity verily leaves a profound impact on the body.

Hoping that you have comprehended everything we have discussed thus far, I shall move on to address another important point. As we are all cognisant, freedom is the ultimate emotion that can be experienced and everybody wishes to live as freely as possible. Although, it is a different matter that man becomes subservient by getting entrapped in faulty teachings and that is why, in today's times, very few people are living in a state of ultimate freedom. But let me state emphatically that people who live in absolute freedom do not succumb to illness easily. Being subservient implies not being able to do what your mind desires, and this is verily the greatest cause of all of man's maladies. Ergo, if your life is fettered by shackles in every aspect, then beware, and if you do not even have the liberty to speak freely or express your feelings, then you are certainly a sitting duck for some terrible ai!ment. That is because, to suppress the mind beyond a limit is not a good habit, and suppressing your thoughts and feelings deep inside can prove to be extremely dangerous. However, many people are naturally habituated to suppressing their thoughts and feelings; they never express themselves completely. Such people must tread carefully, because there is no greater poison than the thoughts and feelings suppressed within the mind. This can even lead to cancer or you might just fall prey to heart disease. Hence, do not suppress your thoughts and feelings as far as possible. If a person is unduly subjugating you, then bestir yourself and stand up to defend yourself with all your might. You are, after all, a human being, so simply do not let yourself be subjugated beyond a point. I am well aware that all the teachings of your communities and the society at large are suppressive in nature, and to make matters worse, even family members are engaged in the monstrous task of overpowering one another. But once you resolve to take a firm stand for yourself, who can dare suppress you, without cause? Besides, safeguarding your own self is verily your primary duty. Thus, never let yourself be suppressed to the extent that you are reduced to stifling even your thoughts and feelings. And if nothing else, at least maintain good, healthy relations with a few close friends with whom you can share your feelings honestly and openly. Engage in any means, but ensure that your words and feelings find a way to vent out, otherwise not only will you age faster than your years but you will also succumb to grave illness.

I am certain, you must have comprehended all the allusions I have made in brief. So, pass a firm resolution to maintain good health and forthwith pen a *Japa Mantra* for yourself in your own words.

Henceforth, accord great importance to safeguarding yourself from mental ailments in order to remain in good health, and as far as possible, do not allow any negative emotion to take root within you. Bask in the sweet air of freedom and endeavour to do whatever it takes to avoid being suppressed as far as possible. Furthermore, on your part, extend others the courtesy of living their lives freely as well and do not try to subjugate anyone. This behaviour of yours will, in turn, safeguard your own freedom, because logically speaking, only if you spare others, will they spare you. The way of the world is, you scratch my back, and I will scratch yours. Ergo, without further ado, compose your *Japa Mantra* in your own words to always remain hale and hearty both in mind and body.

Your *Japa Mantra*

....

....

....

....

....

....

....

Although, even after abiding by all the above rules, bear in mind that the human body is unpredictable as per Nature's design. Consequently, any ailment, both physical as well as mental, can emerge at any time, even in the case of a person who is in the prime of health. Swami Vivekananda is the best example of this phenomenon; he was physically as well as mentally strong, but he nonetheless departed from this world when he was still in his prime. Hence, I advise you to lead your life accepting and embracing this unpredictability of the body so that you are not jolted out of your complacency and suffer from a rude shock at the last moment. At the same time, considering the body's said unpredictability, finish whatever you start in the day, that day itself, for, who knows what tomorrow might bring!

Core Essence of Step 2

Step 2 is an apt solution to cast out all woes and miseries from life; it is the key weapon to attain deliverance from all the negative emotions tormenting you. Ergo, you must utilise it optimally, for, never again will you chance upon such a wonderful opportunity to be liberated from all the ills plaguing your mind. Having said that, it is quite possible that not every person will find it equally easy to imbibe and abide by it, but it is assuredly effective for one and all. For, it is pure and unalloyed spiritual science, and that is precisely why, it is the sole solution to banish all your woes and troubles. There is simply no other recourse that can help you be rid of negativities. Viewed from this perspective, you have now attained a much better understanding of human psychology than almost anybody else, because you have discerned the root cause of all your pains and miseries, which is nothing but establishing a connection with the external world. And the person who has imbibed step 1 sincerely and thoroughly will swiftly and effortlessly put step 2 into practice.

However, before you proceed, you must comprehend an important point in this regard; in no way did you arrive in this world clutching onto these negative emotions. Nature had verily endowed you with a pure mind before sending you in this world. To substantiate this truth, if you walk down the memory lane and take a peek into your childhood, you would recall that neither tension, sorrow, disappointment nor despondency, depression and fear ever overcame you as a child. So, wherefrom did these emotions appear then? Well, regardless of where they may have descended from, you can neither hold me nor God or Nature accountable for it. This begs the question, from where have these negative emotions sneaked into your life? The answer is, all these feelings have stemmed from the knowledge that you have imbibed externally. And from where have you garnered such knowledge? Certainly, from family members, teachers, society and community. And since none of them possess any knowledge either of spiritual science or of Nature's design, all of them, out of sheer ignorance, have taught you to establish a connection with the external world. And eventually, this very connection with the external world became the cause of all your sorrows. So, neither can you place the blame on Nature for your negative emotions nor can you vent your frustration on me. If you wish to hold anyone culpable for your negativities, then take to task the communities, the social system, the education system and your family members. This is the reason I declare that all kinds of teachings can be beneficial if they are combined with and supported by spiritual science, but without the latter, the best of instructions are worth naught. Thus, I request everyone to blend spiritual science into all that they preach and make the principles of Nature's design their boundary, which must not be defied. And if you cannot do so, then seal your lips; otherwise, the venom of negative emotions will continue to spread far and wide. If you cast a look around you, you would see that members of every community are engaged in making lofty declarations; but forget about helping others, are they themselves benefitting from it? The moment you utter something which is at odds with their belief system, all their frustrations spew out in a tirade, culminating into bloodshed and violence. The so-called flag-bearers of the society are no different. The plain truth is, where negative emotions are concerned, the condition of the majority of religious *gurus* and propagators of society is far worse than that of ordinary human beings. Thus, wake up from your slumber and become aware; stop listening to other people or you will continue to be further ensnared in their web, mired in confusion. I have already taught you how to become your own doctor, so simply conduct a thorough and precise surgery on yourself and get delivered from all kinds of negativities for good. And once you do so, you will become eligible to enter step 3, where we will learn how to attain the pinnacle of success, without establishing any connection with the external world. So, simply pass step 2, and then just watch how your life takes a momentous turn.

STEP 3

Have you ever reflected upon the history of humankind? And while pondering over it, have you noticed something special about this vast history spanning millennia? Perhaps not...! For, if you had, your life would not have receded to the state it presently is in. And I base this statement on several reasons that will justify it. First and foremost, in this world, an ordinary human being has access to everything in order to lead a blissful life. He has access to the knowledge propounded by the likes of Krishna, Buddha and Christ for his enlightenment, and a melodious array of soul-stirring songs composed by scores of musicians belonging to various genres for his entertainment. Likewise, to prepare delicious meals replete with nourishment, he has access to numerous recipes, while he has exquisite clothes to attire himself in. He has modern houses replete with all possible comforts and amenities to live in, and he has access to television and movies to lend him entertainment. Besides, he has the facility of availing modern science and technology for his benefit, right from getting a blood test done to having a surgery performed, in the event of him feeling indisposed. House, car, air conditioner, aeroplane, there is, indeed, no end to the comforts and conveniences at his disposal. But where has all this come from? These comforts, amenities and innovations have certainly not dropped from the sky; the primitive human being had none of these conveniences at his disposal. In other words, these have not been granted to man by Nature. Then, from where have all these come into existence? Who has brought all these marvellous creations into being? Well, it is none other than the great visionaries, men and women who have innovated and created these over the years on the strength of their great work. And if today's human being has access to so many options of comforts and entertainment, then he, undoubtedly, owes his comfortable existence to the endeavour of these great people. Now, tell me, how many great beings have graced this world in the past five hundred years? Barely, a few thousand! This implies, only one in thousands is able to attain greatness. And who deserves to be called great? Only those, who with their diligence, create something which leads to the betterment of humankind as a whole; there can simply be no other criteria to define greatness in human beings.

Now, how did this simple thought not occur to you? And in case you have had this thought, why did the notion of attaining greatness not strike you? I will tell you why...because the world has ensnared the ordinary human being in so many pointless tasks and vain knowledge that man finds it well-nigh impossible to aspire to greatness. Never mind! You can at least accept that you have been provided with everything on a platter on account of the labour of these great people. All you have to do, at the most, is make money in order to attain all those comforts and conveniences. But alas, the greater majority of human beings are unable to discharge even this one task in the right manner. This is, indeed, lamentable! Just imagine, when the world abounds with such beauty and grandeur on the strength of just a few thousand human beings attaining greatness, how beautifully the world would blossom if every person born became great? This world of ours will then assuredly surpass all fantasies of heaven. So, when this vision can be a reality, it should certainly be turned into a reality, as each one of us has a right to attain greatness. And there is no roadblock from Nature's end in the path of greatness; history bears testimony to the fact that not only the unlettered and the atheists, but even the people from impoverished backgrounds have scaled the heights of greatness. Furthermore, even those who are physically challenged have performed astounding feats in this world; in other words, as per Nature's design, there is no obstacle for anyone in the path to attaining greatness. Besides, attaining greatness is man's *dharma*, his rightful path, and to create something novel and beneficial for humanity is his sole duty. For, when man is enjoying the creations of thousands of human beings, it verily becomes his bounden duty to reciprocate and give humanity something new and creative in return.

With that said, what is really acting as a hurdle in the path to greatness? Where is everyone faltering? Without beating around the bush, I shall come straight to the point; it is man's brain or his intellect which acts as a barrier, thus, becoming the sole stumbling block to attaining greatness. But nobody realises this fact because even today, there is a grave dearth of psychological knowledge in this world. Never mind! Let me make an allusion in that direction to help you comprehend this point. Actually, man, in his possession, has two key powers to set his life on the path of progress and prosperity. First, his brain, with which everyone is familiar; and second, the mind, about which the preponderance of people are completely in the dark. And when I say mind, I am speaking of the powerful minds, because the weak minds are verily a creation of your own brain. Surprisingly, however, the majority of people in the world are entirely oblivious to the difference between the mind and the brain. Now, if you wish to apprehend this difference and comprehend the mind in its entirety, then you must read my book 'I am the Mind'. Well, let me now apprise you in brief about the powers of the mind and the brain; if nothing else, with this elucidation, you will at least be in the know and get a basic idea of this difference.

Powers of the Brain	Powers of the Mind
1. To think and analyse, to reason and to make calculations are the tasks that fall under the purview of the brain.	1. A human being possesses four powerful minds in total, and they do not engage in any of the tasks undertaken by the brain.

2. The brain arrives at decisions purely on the basis of that which already exists, and this is its limit of functioning.	2. The decisions resulting from the mind's powers are always based on something new and novel.
3. As it is the limitation of the brain to act on the basis of available objects, it makes all its decisions purely based on information and logical reasoning.	3. The mind barely has any need for information. It is so powerful that it can instantaneously express thoughts in a novel way. To do so, all it needs is a hint.
4. Although it can execute mechanical tasks with perfection, the brain is incapable of creativity.	4. The mind cannot perform mechanical tasks. It is addicted to innovative ideas and tasks; hence, every kind of inventiveness and innovation can burst forth only from the mind.
5. As garnering information is the limit of the brain's sphere, it is invariably drawn towards the external world.	5. Aligned with the ultimate powers of Nature, the mind is drawn towards Nature's laws and powers, and with their support, it can perform countless feats of creativity.

In brief, both these powers dwell within you and both are vital in their own way. But if you wish to scale the peak of greatness, then it is imperative to activate the 'mind'. For, a human being's four minds are far more powerful than the brain; the brain has innumerable limitations, but the mind is limitless. The mind has a direct connection with Nature's powers and it is simply impossible to attain greatness without securing the support of Nature's powers. After all, there is a limit to how far one can progress with the aid of man-made knowledge. Despite this, everyone is using man-made knowledge as a crutch, striving to labour towards prosperity, and consequently, everyone remains entrapped in the struggle for even basic amenities such as food, clothing and shelter, all their lives. Whether it is the knowledge prescribed by your community or society, your education system or any other knowledge, they are all conceived by human beings. They can surely aid you to a certain degree, but they cannot be your constant companions who will help cross the many bridges of your life, for, they are incomplete in themselves. Verily, it is Nature's ultimate powers alone which are complete and can assist you in entirety. That is precisely why, the unlettered and the atheists become great, while those who hanker after religion or education spend their lives suffering the blows of life. Honestly speaking, you will not find anybody who speaks more plainly than this. Do not miss this opportunity, for, this is your only chance, so wake up from your somnolence! You must realise that it is imperative for you to activate your mind's powers and procure the assistance of Nature's powers. It is you who has to apprehend that your powerful minds are the only key to unlock the gateway to greatness, and that nothing besides Nature's powers and its laws are God. I have no objection to the word 'God', provided you consider the laws of Nature as God. But ordinarily, this is not the case; every person has drawn his own unique conception of God, and these contrivances are of myriad kinds. Furthermore, none of them have anything to do with the real God, which is why, I avoid employing the word 'God' in the first place. I hope you must have grasped my constraint in this regard.

Indeed, with this explanation, I am certain that the confusions regarding Nature and its ultimate powers have been cleared, and there is no question of anybody harbouring doubts about the authority tending to such a vast universe. And if perchance someone still believes that he can prosper and progress without the aid of such an infinite power, then that, in itself, is a testimony of his ignorance. Sad to state, neither does anybody have much knowledge of Nature's authority, power and its laws nor are the laws of Nature specifically discussed. Everyone is so mired in their own world that they do not even spare a glance towards this subject; also, man is so mesmerised and allured by external attractions that he is entirely oblivious to the ultimate powers of the four powerful minds dwelling within him. In short, the greater majority of people in this world are engaged in steering their life on the path of progress, only on the strength of their brains and the (puny) human knowledge they possess. And they fondly believe that they will prosper, progress and make a mark in this world, just by the aid of their brain. Blinded by ignorance, it never occurs to them that Nature has been governing this universe for billions of years, whereas the antiquity of all human knowledge ranges only between 500 to 5000 years. In that case, how can man-made knowledge help one prosper and progress in life? Besides, it is not aiding anybody's growth either; in fact, blind reliance on man-made knowledge is the prime reason behind everybody's lives going astray. Well, in order to help humankind be rid of this predicament, my new book 'The Laws of Nature' will soon be published; upon reading the book, you will assuredly find it easier to fathom Nature's laws. At present, simply remember that without the assistance of Nature's ultimate powers, there is no way one can steer one's life on the path of progress. And if you wish to consider Nature as *Parmaatma* (the Supreme Soul), then you can say that life cannot prosper and progress without the will of the *Parmaatma*, the Supreme Soul. Now, you may accord Nature any name you wish, but if you desire the assistance of its ultimate powers, then it is imperative for all four of your powerful minds to be active. For, they alone will forge a connection between you and Nature's ultimate powers. Ergo, without further ado, let me briefly acquaint you with the peculiarities of your four powerful minds.

Superconscious Mind

When this mind is active, qualities such as self-confidence, concentration, enthusiasm and perseverance become automatically available at one's disposal. And let me emphasise here, these qualities cannot be acquired if this mind lies dormant; it is this very peculiarity of the Superconscious Mind that elevates it to the highest level and lends importance to it.

Spontaneous Mind

This mind is akin to a computer which analyses (all the) data and provides its result instantaneously. Upon the activation of this mind, not only does man save time, but his decisions also invariably prove to be right. Just think, once the Spontaneous Mind becomes active, who on the face of this earth can stop you from becoming successful?

Collective Conscious Mind

This mind is a computer-like machine, which is connected to the minds of all human beings. That is to say, if this mind is active, you can decipher the mindset of the masses instantaneously. The people with an active Collective Conscious Mind always manage to gauge the mass psychology; they can fathom which product will sell, which movie will turn into a blockbuster at the box office, and what kind of ad copy should be written to lure people to buy a product or service. In other words, the peculiarity of this mind is its ability to discern the mindset of the crowd. Usually, those who have an active Collective Conscious Mind are able to influence the crowd with impeccable ease. All the marketing strategies generated through this mind are always apt, hitting the bull's eye with precision. With these examples, I am sure you must have deciphered why it is imperative for this mind to be active as well.

Ultimate Mind

This mind pulsates in unison with Nature, therefore, a person with an active Ultimate Mind becomes completely aligned with Nature. Then, regardless of what he does, his actions will invariably be right. He will always remain pure and guileless. Esteemed personalities who fall into this category are Buddha, Krishna, Christ and several others belonging to their ilk.

Summarising the discussion so far, I have provided you with a succinct description of your powerful minds and the feats they are capable of performing. With this, you must have surely fathomed that miracles can occur when these minds are active. So, push aside all nonsensical ideas and thoughts, and instead, focus on the teachings which enable the activation of these minds; furthermore, develop a keen interest in true spiritual psychology. I am confident that you will at least make this little effort to set your life on the path of progress.

Proceeding ahead with this tacit assurance, let me ask you, have you ever wondered, what is it that makes a human being attain greatness? In this context, clearly note that powerful and potent emotions such as enthusiasm, self-confidence, concentration, foresight make a man great. And these emotions cannot be experienced as long as the Superconscious Mind remains dormant. So, what is it that acts as a deterrent to the activation of the Superconscious Mind? Flummoxed, are you? Let me reiterate that it is man-made knowledge that acts as a stumbling block in this case. Else, a child is verily born in his Superconscious Mind; and concentration, enthusiasm, self-confidence, enjoyment and similar qualities are his natural state of being. However, you lose them as you grow up, lured into the entanglement of human teachings, and subsequently find yourself ensnared in the web of the three weak minds, namely your Conscious Mind, Unconscious Mind and Subconscious Mind, which choke your life with misery, worry, fear, despondency, depression and other negative emotions. Unfortunately, even those who deliver speeches or write tomes on psychology are completely oblivious to the fact that a human being has seven minds. In their ignorance, they also hold the belief that, at best, a human being has two minds; one, the weak mind which is termed as the conscious mind and the other, the powerful mind which is known as the subconscious mind. But if you wish to experience the presence of all seven minds existent within you, then it is best that you read my book 'I am the Mind'. This book will be of great help in activating your powerful minds, and besides, it will also teach you the right way to rear children, for, as I have stated earlier, a child is verily born in his Superconscious Mind. Ergo, even if you are unable to do anything for yourself, at least establish a rock-solid foundation in order to pave the way for a beautiful life for your child. This is the reason I am emphasising this point and am compelled to ask you to read this book ever so often.

After having progressed in the discussion so far, you must have at least comprehended the fact that without the activation of your powerful minds and sans Nature's guidance, your life shall remain bereft of progress and prosperity. Step 1 and step 2 are the very foundations to activate your powerful minds and help you connect with Nature. Actually, every human being in this world, fettered with man-made knowledge and external attractions, has become a circus lion, whereas Nature had originally sent everybody into this world as a mighty king of the forest. But unfortunately, everybody has lost the crown they had once worn; instead, they have learnt to match their steps to the sound of the whip. Only a handful few have been able to save themselves from becoming a circus lion; some on account of good upbringing, while others by virtue of their pertinacity and perseverance. The rest have enrolled themselves in the circus devised by human knowledge; and thereafter, numerous ringmasters have entered their lives bearing stinging whips, forcing them to perform one trick after another, at the sound of every whip. In other words, life became synonymous with compulsion and slavery, and a slave bound by compulsions can barely achieve anything in life! Step 1, therefore, aims to embolden you, making you more independent, and also teaches you to reclaim the reins of your life and become alive again. It also teaches you to guard yourself religiously, helping you break free from the fetters of bondage. The one who has imbibed the practical applications of step 1 with all sincerity must have assuredly experienced a personality transformation, and let me tell you that only a person whose personality has transformed, can enter step 2.

Next, let us discuss the impact of step 2 on your psyche. The objective of step 2 is to deliver you from all kinds of vain knowledge devised by human beings. For, the root of all your pains and sorrows is nothing save for establishing unnecessary connections with the external world, by getting entangled in all sorts of man-made knowledge. Step 2 aims to break these very connections that you have forged knowingly or unknowingly. And the moment one gets liberated from pains and sorrows, life invariably becomes beautiful, all at once, and if life is beautiful, then it is ready to take flight, soaring on the wings of freedom. So, step 1 and step 2 are the foundations that prepare you for this flight, because futile human knowledge has completely entangled everyone in its bewildering labyrinth. Forget soaring to the sky, even treading on the ground without stumbling has become an onerous task. Futile man-made knowledge has made people believe that one will attain peace and tranquillity only when one achieves success in all spheres of life. And everybody jumps into the fray of attaining success in this manner, thereby entering a grind which haunts them until they depart from this world. As a result, let alone success, even leading an ordinary life seems burdensome. Unfortunately, almost everybody has been reduced to this pathetic state, because they fail to comprehend that the design of Nature is completely at variance with such petty human knowledge. That is why, Kabir calls this world an upturned flute. In Nature's design, in order to attain any kind of success, man has to first dispel his pains and sorrows, and whoever succeeds in doing so, becomes entitled to soar on a magnificent flight. That is why, true spiritual science accords importance to happiness, peace, joy, contentment and so on. And, pray tell, why does it place emphasis upon these? The simple reason is, if life abounds with happiness, peace and similar positive emotions, then it verily implies that it is free of woes and sorrows. And as you well know, stress and joy cannot co-exist. But ironically, people worry that if they live peacefully and contentedly, they will not prosper and progress, or that they will not make great strides in life if they do not worry or struggle. But as per the design of Nature, only a person with a serene mindset, whose life abounds with joy and happiness, is entitled to phenomenal success. In other words, greatness and success is the ultimate goal for both man-made knowledge and Nature, but there is a fundamental difference between the two. Man-made knowledge presumes that if one attains success, then life will always abound with happiness and peace, whereas as per the law of Nature, if you lead a happy and contented life, then success is bound to grace your life. In other words, both approaches aim for happiness and success, but they are at variance as to what should be attained first. But most certainly, the laws of Nature will emerge victorious in this tussle; there can be no doubt about it! That is why, spiritual science emphasises upon alleviating pains and sorrows, but human knowledge does not concur with this approach. Human knowledge promises deliverance from woes and sorrows and a life abounding with happiness and peace, if you attain a certain status and material possessions. And man, being naïve as he is, having hopelessly fallen for such vain declarations, has reduced his life to a mad race, wherein both success as well as happiness and peace elude him.

In essence, you must comprehend that dispelling pains and sorrows is the only straightforward way to attain success; besides, a man living a life free of pains and sorrows is, at any rate, successful. For, how can a person whose life thrives with happiness, merriment and peace be termed a failure? Ergo, upon passing step 2, a person invariably attains success for himself. Once he has achieved this success, all that remains is attaining success as per the world's terminology. To accomplish this, Nature and your powerful minds together perpetually guide you towards the path you must tread for attaining material progress and prosperity. In modern parlance, life is akin to an aeroplane, wherein it is the pilot's responsibility to lift the aircraft to a certain height, and thereafter, put it on autopilot. The same rule applies to life, wherein a human being has to simply eliminate pains and sorrows from his life, and thereafter Nature grabs hold of him. Then, all subsequent responsibility is shouldered by Nature and man's powerful minds, who collectively lead him towards greatness. You simply have to comprehend that attaining greatness without activating one's powerful minds, in the absence of the grace of Nature, is well-nigh impossible. Thus, those who have passed step 2 can consider themselves wholly prepared to take flight. Although, I am aware that passing step 2 is no mean feat, for, the greater majority of mankind is sunk knee-deep in this vain, illusory quagmire...However, once you have cleared step 1, progressing to step 2 would not be so difficult either. I am confident that come what may, you will all certainly clear step 2, and will break free from the shackles of woes and sorrows post-haste. For that matter, you ought to make this little effort in order to set your life on the path of progress. And I am sanguine that you will do so successfully.

Well, another pertinent point that demands reflection on your part is, what lies at the root of all of man's failures? The root cause is, he is unable to perform to the best of his capability. He certainly does not lack talent, but not being able to showcase one's talent in the best possible manner is, undoubtedly, a problem beleaguering every human being. What then is the reason behind this? Well, the reason is, he is mired in sorrows, miseries and tensions, and it is common knowledge that one's performance suffers when one is under duress and stress. Perhaps, the point I wish to emphasise can be better borne out by citing the example of the battle of Mahabharata. Arjuna was popularly known as one of the finest archers of his time, but moments before the battle commenced, he was overcome by the nerve-wracking anxiety of 'what will happen'. Reduced to a pathetic state, he apprised Krishna that his skin is burning all over, his mouth has run dry, and he can only see omens of misfortune looming in the distance. Furthermore, he says that he is incapable of even lifting his bow! In other words, the finest of archers, who could normally slay his enemies in thousands, becomes incapable of lifting his own bow. Just think about the pathetic state a single tension had reduced Arjuna to! And what decoy did Krishna employ to cast away Arjuna's tension? He did not teach Arjuna to lift or wield the bow, because the latter was far better skilled than Krishna in archery. Ergo, Krishna dispelled Arjuna's tension, and no sooner was Arjuna rid of his tension than he attained victory in the Mahabharata war and annihilated the gigantic army of the Kauravas. I am certain, you are all talented people and you must assuredly be performing countless tasks, much more effectively and efficiently than me. Hence, I am not tutoring you on how to perform in your field of speciality, but I am showing you the path to dispel your tension so that you can demonstrate your talent at its best. And step 2 was designed with the very objective of banishing all your tensions.

Lastly, you need to bear in mind that steps 1 and 2 require you to become your own doctor; that is precisely what I had taught you. But step 3 is entirely different; here, you have to bow out of your role as your doctor. In this step, you do not have to do anything for yourself, but accept the refuge of your powerful minds and Nature. Hereon, those two will collectively undertake all the important tasks which ought to be done, and similarly, every key decision will be made with their consensus. After passing step 2 with flying colours, you would no longer be a slave to man-made knowledge, for now, your brain and ego are rendered powerless to do anything of consequence. It is 'Nature and your powerful minds' that will now hold sway over your brain as well as your bodily functions. For, as soon as you clear step 2, you become a child of Nature. Now, the reins of all your future births are in its hands alone, and you will remain wonderstruck by the astonishing feats that Nature will now perform through your powerful minds. Simply comprehend, if you let anybody else become your doctor in steps 1 and 2, then you will indubitably fail to clear those steps; however, step 3 is the exact opposite. Here, if you try to become your own doctor, you will fail miserably. In this step, your total and absolute surrender is crucial, because from now on, only Nature and your powerful minds are the doctors of your life.

On this note, let me shed light on another profound point related to spiritual science. The approach of spiritual science is to settle your mind and align it with Nature. Everything else that follows then transpires in a seamless flow, all by itself. But all of this occurs in two stages, as two kinds of human beings dwell in this world. One are those who are ensnared in the illusory trap of the world, and second are those who have risen above it. Consider this book itself as an example. Here, step 1 and step 2 are for those who have fallen prey to worldly attractions, whereas step 3 is for those who have attained the freedom of their mind. Ergo, both points will perforce have to be made separately. In steps 1 and 2, I will but have to ask you to become your own doctor, because you are presently no better than a slave, but in step 3, I am assuming that you are no longer languishing under any kind of servitude. Thus, as far as step 3 is concerned, I am asking you to surrender yourself and simply give up any attempt to become your own doctor. Now, at first, both these points will seem contradictory, but in actuality, they are one and the same. It is imperative to make the same point using two different approaches, because human beings are living in either of the aforementioned two stages. Thus, henceforth, whenever you read any apt text based on spiritual science, be assured that it will contain contradictions, and come to think of it, the Bhagavad Gita is no exception to it either. Because when Arjuna sinks down to the nadir of despair, Krishna's words carry a different meaning, but when Arjuna tears through the veil of gloom and rises up, Krishna's words have an altogether different import than what he had stated earlier. I am stating this here, because man often fails to comprehend the profundity of spiritual science. He finds himself unable to apprehend the contradictory points, and eventually, he finds it impossible to move ahead, remaining tangled in those contradictions. So, henceforth, whenever you read any profound spiritual science, know that it will certainly have contradictory statements, and only if you learn to connect with both the statements, will you be able to comprehend them in their entirety. Remember, it is only ignoramuses who make one-sided statements, and that is precisely why, you find yourself easily falling prey to their words. With this, I have taught you the method of comprehending spiritual science and I hope, from now onwards, you will be able to correctly imbibe all the knowledge based in spiritual science.

Proceeding further, I will now provide you with some practical applications of step 3, and elucidate how you can use them to derive utmost benefit from your powerful minds. At the same time, I will show you how, with the aid of these powerful minds, you can entrust the reins of your life to Nature's ultimate authority. There is one hitch though; only the ones who have actually passed step 2 and have truly severed all meaningless connections, will be able to benefit from the practical applications of step 3. For, only then will you be able to entrust your life to Nature's ultimate authority. And the ultimate authority of Nature does not function in accordance with human devised knowledge. It elevates a seemingly ordinary boy who spent his days working as a pump attendant to the pinnacle of success, thereby making him the business magnate Dhirubhai Ambani. It transforms a barely educated Edison into an inventor who registered over a thousand patents, and it turns Bill Gates, who believed neither in God nor destiny, into a world-renowned personality. So, all said and done, this ultimate authority is extremely powerful, but it will not accept you the way you are presently; only the person who has passed step 2 completely, will be accorded this opportunity. Ergo, I will first provide you with a few tests, through which you can gauge the extent to which you have succeeded in passing step 2, and only then will I speak of the practical applications of step 3.

Tests to Gauge Eligibility for Step 3

1. You must have begun to abound with positivity

Well, to begin with, steps 1 and 2 are nothing but surgeries to establish you in your Superconscious Mind once again, or to put it succinctly, they are the means by which you regain the mindset you had in your childhood. As stated earlier, every child is born in the Superconscious Mind and an array of positive emotions naturally dwell in that mind. Furthermore, this mind is free of all kinds of negative emotions and that is precisely why, you will never encounter a child who is worried, frustrated, sad or disappointed. Every child you meet is invariably bubbling with joy, merriment, peace and energy; and perseverance, enthusiasm, concentration and confidence are verily the natural qualities of all children. Indeed, it is beyond me how you can lose such an utterly precious treasure and become entrapped in the web of negative emotions. You must comprehend that by succumbing to faulty teachings, you lose your positivity, and subsequently become compelled to lead a life rife with negativities. But upon successfully graduating from steps 1 and 2, you will once again be ensconced in the childlike state of your childhood; you will abound with happiness, enjoyment, confidence, concentration and joy. And only when you have transformed into such a person, should you consider that you have cleared steps 1 and 2.

Now, the question you may well ask is, why is it essential to regain a child-like mind? Simply because, without doing so, nothing of consequence shall ever transpire in life. Indeed, numerous declarations of spiritual science must have surely fallen upon your ears, but perhaps, you must have disregarded them. Oftentimes, you must have heard the words of Christ, wherein he declared that only those who are like children would be able to enter his kingdom. Now, can you tell me, which kingdom is Christ talking about in this context? Undoubtedly, the kingdom of Nature; the kingdom of the Supreme Soul. And what is the peculiarity of that kingdom? It is a place where nothing but happiness and success prevails. But the question that follows next is, who will be able to enter that kingdom? Christ states, only the person who is child-like! I am sure you must have deciphered now why I wish to turn you into a child once again. Likewise, you must have heard that children are nurtured by the Supreme Soul; here, the Supreme Soul denotes Nature. And this statement is absolutely true! That is precisely why, a child abounds with all kinds of positive emotions. Nonetheless, pseudo-intellectuals who are wont to propagate ludicrous ideas take the onus of carrying out this deed, snatching it away from (the able hands of) Nature. And it is from this very point that life starts sliding off the right track. But it is still not too late! Steps 1 and 2 are the means to entrust your life in the hands of Nature once again. And do you know, what will follow once Nature takes over the reins of your life? Enjoyment, happiness and success will cascade in a torrent, suffusing your life with its many-splendoured hues!

Nevertheless, I have one more request to make at this juncture. If you have comprehended the vital point stated above, then kindly safeguard your children from falling into the illusory trap of vain teachings. Because, the person, whose reins of life remain in the hands of the Supreme Soul right from childhood, is bound to attain greatness. Having made this crucial point, let me come back to you. I am sure you must have attained a child-like mind, having passed steps 1 and 2, and you are now ready to take off on a great and memorable flight.

2. You must have regained control over your life

After having cleared steps 1 and 2, you must have certainly become your own master. Furthermore, you must assuredly be experiencing utmost freedom and you must have also experienced deliverance from all kinds of bondages. Now, you may wonder, what is the proof of all these changes having occurred in your life? Well, the plain and simple proof is, your concentration in work must have increased significantly and your life must have become much happier and merrier than before. Also, you must have started safeguarding your interests and wishes suitably, or if stated differently, rather than quashing them, you are now able to give a free vent to your interests and desires. If all these changes have transpired within you, then know for sure that you have passed steps 1 and 2 with flying colours.

3. You should live and feel like a 'king'

This is the most crucial test of whether or not you have really passed steps 1 and 2. If you have cleared these steps, then you must have started considering yourself no less than a king. And what is the definition of a king? He is the master of his universe, a person who has everything in the world that he should have. And let me tell you that experiencing this kingliness is a state of mind, and not a physical state. It would be erroneous to surmise that a person who possesses material wealth and fame is a king. No, absolutely not, this couldn't be further from the truth...the kingliness I am referring to is all about a person's mindset. If I believe that I am the king, then I am, indeed, the king. Then, it doesn't matter even if I don't possess a penny to my name. And in your childhood, you were, undoubtedly, a king. As a child, you were not dependent on a fancy car to lend you status; racing an inexpensive toy car on the street, you believed yourself to be the king of the world, didn't you? Similarly, as a child, your happiness did not hinge upon a big house; playing in the mud for hours would bring endless joy to you. Likewise, you were not dependent on religious practices to be termed religious; instead, you attained the peace and contentment of being religious just by doing whatever you did as a child. Ergo, if you have passed steps 1 and 2 in the right manner, then you would have become that kind of a king once again.

Having said that, what does being a king imply? Only the belief that 'I possess everything!' So, what does possessing everything signify? Just that, 'I want nothing more. Whatever I have and whatever state it may be in, it is so perfect that I can spend the rest of my days merrily, with a smile on my lips and a song in my heart.' Verily, only a person with such a mindset can be called a true king. As for the question of attaining everything is concerned, nobody can ever attain it all nor can anyone ever become everything. But yes, one can certainly lead one's life wearing the dignity of being a king, with the belief that one has everything. And it is this very notion of being a king irrespective of the circumstances, which is called 'contentment' in the lexicon of spiritual science. Furthermore, spiritual science declares that contentment is the ultimate wealth of a human being, priceless and invaluable, and that there can be no wealth greater than contentment in this world. Indeed, this is the absolute truth! But having fallen into the trap of human ignorance, man agonises, 'How will I make progress if I become satisfied with my lot and live in contentment?' It is for this very reason that human ignorance stresses upon effectuating wishes and ambitions. Now, the question arises, what will set life on the path of progress—contentment or ambitions and desires? Take a look around you, everyone is nursing wishes and ambitions, but how many lives are getting set? Next to none! That is because, desire and ambition signify that 'I will decide what I want and what I wish to become.' And, this 'I' verily denotes 'the ego'. And what is the stature of man's 'I', his (puny) ego before Nature's ultimate authority? Why, nothing at all...and that is exactly why, everybody in this world is worried and vexed. On the other hand, contentment denotes lack of desires; it implies that Nature is far better cognisant than me of what I should possess and what I should become. Therefore, let it grant me and take away from me whatever it wills and let it shape me into whoever it wants me to be; I will simply go on living my life, merrily and contentedly. In brief, desires and ambitions symbolise the ego and are an attempt to force one's will upon Nature's, which is simply impossible, while contentment signifies dedicating one's life to Nature. And this is exactly what step 3 teaches you: to dedicate your entire life to Nature and to embrace the belief that I leave it in Nature's hands to decide what I should or should not receive in life. Neither do I have to contemplate or rack my brain over it, nor do I have to nurse a desire. And, worrying about anything is simply out of the question, for, I have handed over the reins of my life in the able hands of Nature.

Comprehend this clearly that the above-mentioned mindset is essential for attaining any kind of historic success because only then, does Nature get an opportunity to step into your life, allowing your powerful minds to become active once again. Thereafter, these two together continue to perform ever more marvellous feats in your life. All you have to do is observe faith and patience; the moment you lose either quality, you will simultaneously lose your kingliness. Then, you will no longer remain a contented person. Because, faith and patience are the keystones of the natural state of being of a satisfied and contented person; for, faith and patience are but another form of contentment. This is the marked feature of many sayings of countless, wise men who have staunchly emphasised on the virtues of practising faith and patience. In a nutshell, if all the above-mentioned mindsets are not present within you, then know that you have still not rightly passed steps 1 and 2. Thus, even if this is the case, there is no cause for worry, for, the illusory trap of human ignorance runs so deep that it might very well take some time to extricate yourself from the mire. Slacken not your efforts, but make persistent efforts to pass steps 1 and 2, and experience the feeling of being a king once again under any circumstances, because only then, will you be able to dedicate yourself to Nature. Nature's grace is never bestowed upon the paupers who continue to demand one thing after another. Nature doesn't consider them worthy of even a glance. That is verily why, such people are reduced to a pathetic state, wherein they keep yearning and wishing throughout their life, but they achieve nothing of significance. Sorrows and tensions continue dogging their footsteps until one day, they finally depart from this world in a morose state. So, neither ask nor wish for anything; just experience the feeling of kingship in whatever you have, regardless of the state it may be in, and Nature will embrace you in its loving arms.

If you still find something lacking and haven't experienced kingliness in its full glory, then pass a firm resolution in your own words to awaken the belief that you are a king. And then, repeat it like a *Japa Mantra* whenever required, because doing so will bridge whatever little distance is still left to traverse in order to attain the mindset of a king.

Your *Japa Mantra*

....

....

....

....

....

....

....

....

Give due respect to your mindset of being a king

If you are truly experiencing the state of kingship, then you must respect this mindset of yours, because only one in thousands is able to attain this loftiness of the mind. And the day is not far when you will join the ilk of the legends. If truth be told, the feeling of 'I do not wish for anything, everything is just perfect,' is in itself a great achievement, and only a person who has experienced this kingship can gauge the joy this contentment brings. All other joys of the world pale in comparison to this joy, and that is bound to be, for now you are under the direct care of Nature. You no longer need to worry about yourself, because Nature has cast its benevolent gaze on your life, and Nature is far more interested in your life than you yourself are, because after all, you have surrendered your life to it. Therefore, Nature is far more eager than you to bring to fruition some great work for the betterment of humanity, using you as a medium. That is why, I am urging you to respect your mindset of kingship; regardless of the upheavals that occur in the external world, do not lose this mindset of kingship under any circumstances. All you need to do is take care of this aspect, and as for the rest, it will be taken care of by Nature.

Furthermore, you must also apprehend the ultimate power of this mindset. Arjuna, in the Bhagavad Gita, is eager to know about this very mindset when he asks Krishna about the traits of a *stithpragya yogi*, a devotee with a steady mindset. To which Krishna responds, such a *yogi* traverses only in his soul, accepts only his soul's orders and also undertakes tasks purely for his soul. Ergo, he forever remains content in his soul alone. He persistently harbours the feeling that there is no king greater than him, because he verily possesses everything which he should. He believes he has all the comforts and conveniences of the world, and he is also replete with knowledge and science. Indeed, it is vital to garner this understanding; for, not only does a person dwelling in this state become distanced from the worldly race but he also keeps well away from all futile knowledge, learning and comprehension. For, he now has the powers of the mind ready to assist him and the benefaction of Nature's ultimate authority to guide him. Consequently, his dependence upon the world is simply out of the question. And this is what Krishna is implying when he tells Arjuna, 'O Arjuna! Even at present, you wish to determine whether or not to fight, by weighing your decision on the scales of victory-vanquishment and virtue-sin. But the decisions of the *yogis* are not contingent upon external circumstances; not only do all their actions spring forth from the soul, but they undertake all their deeds for the soul alone.' Here, also grasp that by soul, Krishna is referring to the powerful minds, which are aligned with Nature. Simply stated, if you have become a *yogi*, who is unaffected by any matter or object, then you can consider yourself to be *stithpragya* (one with a steady mind). If all your actions are stemming from within and if every task you perform leaves you gratified and contented, then know yourself to be a true ascetic with a steady mind. And pray tell, is there anything that can worry a steady-minded person? Of course, there isn't! He has entrusted his entire life to Nature and when his life is functioning as per Nature's desire, then Nature will worry about every upheaval that befalls him. Why will the one with a steady mind be the least bit concerned about any of it? Verily, this is the miracle of this mindset...to be free of worries forever...

Making an allusion to this very mindset of a human being, the great Chinese philosopher, Lao Tzu, pronounces that a person dwelling in this mindset can discern all the mysteries of the universe, without ever glancing out of the window. In other words, no sooner you attain this mindset than you become a genius; and a perspicacious sense, having the capacity to discern any matter in moments, kindles within you. And such a 'sense' is bound to awaken in you because you are now dwelling in the powerful minds, which are directly connected with Nature—the only one cognisant of everything. I believe, you must have now certainly realised the power of the ultimate authority of Nature. So, now, I will give you a few practical applications which will help you reap the benefits of the powers of your mind. Moreover, I will provide you with a few practical applications to attain the benediction of Nature's ultimate authority, which will help you to not only lead a stress-free life, but also to ascend the summit of success. Nevertheless, I will reiterate, only the person who has actually passed steps 1 and 2 will be able to benefit from these practical applications. And even if you have not been able to pass these steps yet, there is no need to worry because by now, you must have certainly progressed by leaps and bounds on this journey. Besides, this is your own scripture and it will always stay with you. So, continue to persevere without pause; if not today, then in the near future, you will assuredly clear steps 1 and 2. And even if you have passed the first two steps to a certain extent, you will still be able to relate with the practical applications ahead. In short, comprehend that you are seated on the ultimate crest of the world and you have procured the assistance of the world's ultimate power. In view of this, all these applications will also be profound in nature. So, imbibe them slowly and peacefully and lay down the foundation to a magnificent and beautiful life. Simply comprehend that after passing steps 1 and 2, you are no longer an ordinary human being, whose life revolves around trivial matters and petty necessities. Now, you are a settled human being, ensconced in the lap of the highest authority, who, irrespective of the measure of his material possessions, experiences the pride of being a king; needless to say, it is kings of this kind whom Nature seeks out and directs towards greatness. As people of this ilk can neither be shaken by hardships nor can they be distressed by sorrows. Obviously, the lives of great people are not adorned with a bower of flowers; they still face their share of struggles. But what makes them stand them apart from the milieu is, they are not bogged down by life's struggles, for, they no longer perceive struggles as struggles, but opportunities to grow in life.

The next point you need to comprehend is, who is able to achieve this greatness? Indeed, it is only a person who allows his creative juices to flow and makes his imprint with innovativeness. Certainly, creativity does not pour forth without the grace of Nature, and Nature invariably showers its blessings only upon the kings. Then, it becomes irrelevant what pursuit the king is involved in or what his possessions are. And nobody is ever too late to exude creativity; no sooner you attain a king-like mindset than Nature chooses you as a medium to undertake a creative task. For instance, Dhirubhai Ambani was a petrol pump attendant, working at a petrol station. But he was content like a king, immersed in that work itself. Hence, not only did Nature teach him everything he had to learn, but it also made him creative and innovative. He did not have to go anywhere to learn anything, be it management or finance or even company laws. Because no sooner did he experience the feeling of kingliness than his natural sense was triggered into complete wakefulness. And natural sense has no necessity to know or study anything externally; it has the capability of comprehending everything in the blink of an eye. The slightest of indications are enough for a human being's natural sense to grasp whatever is worth knowing. And we all know the outstanding feats which Dhirubhai Ambani demonstrated in the capital market. Not only was he an expert in product branding, but his business selection was also remarkably innovative. Similarly, several other stalwarts who shone in their respective fields—from Edison, Walt Disney to Steve Jobs—hailed from impoverished backgrounds, but every one of them was a king at heart. That is why, they were embraced by Nature, and consequently, miracles manifested in their lives in succession. They (automatically) learnt all that they needed to learn and went on to perform one outstanding creative task after another. In short, all I want you to comprehend is, it is not too late for you even now; simply attain the mindset of kingliness and everything else will occur of its own accord.

With the above discussion, you must have surely gauged that the goal of step 3 is to lead you to greatness. And in order to attain greatness, you will verily have to wait for creativity to flow forth, because attaining greatness without creativity is simply impossible. Ergo, all the initial applications of step 3 will deal solely with creativity. All you need to do is imbibe them thoroughly and sincerely, and focus on laying down the foundation to greatness. Furthermore, faith and patience are implicitly the key necessities here. But remember, do not nurse the desire to attain greatness, else this wonderful chance will slip away from your hands. For, as soon as you start harbouring desires, Nature will step back and rescind its blessings. In simple words, you have to dwell in a continuous state of being a king under any circumstances, entrusting everything else to Nature. Make a solemn pledge to yourself that, 'Nature is free to make of me whatever it wills, and it can employ any means it deems fit to achieve this end. I will not lament or protest when faced with any highs and lows in this path, and if troubles befall me, then so be it.' Know this in no uncertain terms that, no sooner you lose your kingliness than you lose your chance to attain greatness as well. Having said that, I am aware that it is not in everyone's power to tread this path and that is precisely why, not everyone can become great. Nevertheless, I am here to hold your hand and guide you despite the limitations, and take you with me on the path to kingliness. So, imbibe the practical applications provided herewith pertaining to creativity; for, they are sure to work wonders...

Applications for Creativity – A Precursor to Greatness

1. Give Your Creativity a Chance to Flow Forth

All of us are cognisant of the fact that despite making incessant efforts to achieve greatness, only one in thousands is able to become great. Do you have any idea why this is so? There is but one reason for it; only one in the milieu of thousands is able to engage in some creative pursuit, and nothing except for creativity can lend greatness to a human being. Regardless of the field, one can attain greatness only when one does something creative. If Krishna and Buddha have attained greatness, it is only because they enunciated new ideologies and tenets, contrary to the prevalent scriptures. Picasso and Van Gogh are successful only because they created enchanting works of art which were unique masterpieces in themselves. Einstein and Newton are household names because they gave radical principles, and likewise, Bill Gates and Steve Jobs are world-renowned personalities for the simple reason that they made innovative inventions catering to people's needs. Here, you must also comprehend what innovative and creative implies; creative denotes that which nobody has ever done before.

This begs the question, where will creativity emerge from? Also, why only one in thousands holds the spark to harness this creativity? Well, you can only hold futile human knowledge accountable for this, falling prey to which, man permits external knowledge to enter within. He fails to comprehend that every bit of information one takes in from the outside world is nothing save for empty information, because these are all statements which have already been uttered, followed or heeded to. And such declarations can never lead you to greatness; they can certainly provide you with a mechanical life, but they cannot make you creative. Such declarations can definitely make your day-to-day life easier, but they cannot lend you greatness. It is only creativity which lends an aura of greatness to a person, which imperatively blooms within and gushes out in a resplendent tapestry of uniqueness. If one were to observe keenly, two kinds of teachings are prevalent in this world. The first kind prompts one to take in knowledge from the outside world, which is what the greater majority of humankind has been perpetually engaged in since aeons. Consequently, nothing novel and unique flows from within them. But for the second kind, who are able to successfully shield themselves from external attractions, creativity surges forth from within them, and one day, that very creativity leads them to greatness.

Now, those of you who have properly imbibed steps 1 and 2 would have certainly realised that everything precious that we possess, dwells within us. This begs the question, how does one activate one's inner voice? Indubitably, there is only one solution to this: liberate oneself from futile external knowledge. If you comprehend carefully, you will realise, this is exactly what I have made you do in step 2. I have severed all your external connections and have rid you of all the futile external knowledge that you had accumulated. Because only once the dirt and grime is cleared away, will the *Kohinoor*, the precious diamond, shine through in all its brilliance! Thus, this treasure, in the form of creativity, will emanate from anyone who has passed step 2. Although it is quite easy to gather nonsensical information from the outside world and establish a connection with it, to rid oneself of it is, indeed, a herculean task. That is why, many people may find step 2 exacting. But if you wish for some great creativity to flow forth through your existence, you will surely have to pass step 2.

To aid you in your endeavour, let me elucidate the significance of step 2 with the example of the eminent scholar, Swami Vivekananda. As we are all in the know, Swami Vivekananda, even as a youth, was incredibly sharp, bright and talented; but he was also very vain about his talents and intelligence. One day, he happened to encounter the great saint, Ramakrishna Paramhansa. No sooner did he meet him than a miracle of the most profound nature manifested itself; he was struck dumb and dazed upon listening to the saint, because he realised that what he considered as knowledge was actually nothing but idle wanderings of the mind. All that knowledge which made him so conceited was not worth a penny and there was only one solution available to him...to unlearn everything that he had learnt. In fact, Vivekananda stated once that he had to strive very hard to unlearn all that he had learnt previously, but because he was a persevering man, he had eventually succeeded in erasing all the futile external knowledge he had accumulated. And as soon as he had succeeded in liberating himself from the limiting shackles of futile knowledge, creativity sprung forth from within him. The magnificent discourse he gave on 'zero' in the USA is verily a proof of his great creativity but remember, it surged forth from within him only when he had rid himself of futile teachings.

In short, all you need to comprehend from this example is, everything of value that you possess lies well within you; not just your happiness, but your knowledge and intelligence also lie within you. Why should you then establish external connections to attain them? For ages, spiritual science has been pronouncing that even your God lies within you. So, firstly, resolve that 'From this day onwards, my inner self will be the beacon that I shall follow, rather than the meaningless noise of the outside world.' And to that end, pass a practical resolution, writing it in your own words. This *Japa Mantra* written by you will serve as a protective shield, safeguarding you from futile external knowledge, and only then will the possibility of creativity emitting from within get kindled. Ergo, in order to become great, firstly imbibe this basic practical application. From this day onwards, start according more importance to your inner self, instead of vain external nonsense.

Your *Japa Mantra*

....

....

....

....

....

....

....

2. Choose a Vocation or Career Path of Your Choice

Indeed, I need not reiterate that everything of value that you possess lies within you, and you are not particularly dependent on the outside world for anything. In that case, you have to let your inner self determine your vocation as well. Indubitably, every person gets a nudge from within in order to undertake certain tasks, and he also derives enjoyment when he performs those tasks. But, entangled in the web of external attractions and pressures, he promptly forgets about them and goes on seeking ever-new vocations. He finds himself vacillating between different careers, lured by the baits dangled before him, either in the form of increased monetary benefits or high demand of the particular vocation. Some people, on the other hand, are burdened with family pressures, while others yield to the pressure of the education system. Subsequently, they choose their career giving in to external influences, abandoning their true calling emanating from within. And let me tell you, this is the point where man gets well and truly ensnared. The greater majority of people have chosen a contrary career path, suppressing the one emerging naturally from within them. You must comprehend that the interest in a particular field that emanates from within is verily the field in which you enjoy performing tasks; in fact, your mind is also able to diligently focus on those very tasks and that is where your talent truly lies. And, one day, by following your true calling, some great creativity is destined to burst forth from within you, in that very field. But unfortunately, only one in thousands is succeeding in establishing himself in the field of his talent, while everyone else is choosing their vocation based on external attractions or pressures, and in this process, they end up severing their precious connection with Nature. Consequently, neither are they able to focus on their task nor do they derive any enjoyment from it. Moreover, all possibilities of creativity emanating from within them also dwindle to naught. For, creativity will flow only from the field chosen by your inner self, and that creativity alone will lead you to greatness.

I hope, you must have thoroughly comprehended all that has been discussed in the preceding paragraphs. We are now in the concluding stage of this book, so you will be able to apprehend my words even if I speak in allusions. Thus, comprehend clearly that Nature has sent you in this world, equipping your inner self with everything that you need. All you need to do is, make your inner self your topmost priority and attain greatness. Let your inner self take the crucial decision of choosing your career path, and then behold the amazing feats you perform! To impress upon you the import of my words, let me explain this point to you with the examples of a few exalted personalities who have left their imprint in the sands of time. Music, for Mozart, had stemmed forth from within; likewise, Edison had chosen the field of science as his vocation by heeding to his inner voice. Similarly, Walt Disney had chosen painting as his career based on the nudge from his inner self, accepting it as a sign from Nature. In fact, not just a few but all great people, without exception, have verily chosen their vocations, by heeding the voice of their inner self.

Therefore, you too must seek your vocation within yourself. Creativity will emerge only from a field chosen by your inner self, as you will be able to focus and enjoy in that field alone. And if nothing else, at least allow your children to choose their vocation by encouraging them to heed their inner voice. Do this small kindness to your children so that they can confidently march ahead in life, treading the right path ordained for them since childhood. By granting them this leeway, you can help them completely bypass steps 1 and 2 and directly dive into step 3 to attain greatness. And as far as you are concerned, it is not too late for you even now. Know that nobody in this world ever misses the boat, because it is verily the miracle of Nature that it is never too late to mend. Thus, as soon as you clear steps 1 and 2, you will experience a great surge in creativity emanating from within you, and if age and energy permit, you can still perform miracles with their assistance. Simply compose your own *Japa Mantra* to that effect and then sit in solitude, close your eyes and continue to repeat that *Japa Mantra*. By reciting it over and over again, creativity will gush forth from within. And, as an initial step, you will begin undertaking all your present tasks with far greater creativity; for, whether it is business or management, there is an efflux of creative feats in each and every field in today's world. Besides, you have performed countless creative feats in your childhood as well; so, by engaging in this exercise, the creativity lying latent within you will also begin to spring forth once again. And if nothing else, this creativity stemming from within will at least accord you the satisfaction of living a worthwhile life. But come what may, do not rest until you have initiated the process of allowing what is inside you to flow forth in the external world. You have already suppressed yourself a great deal by choking yourself with nugatory things from the external world. Moving forward, it would be best if you put an end to this destructive habit. Therefore, pass a firm resolution for the same and pen your *Japa Mantra*.

Your *Japa Mantra*

....

....

....

....

....

3. Shield Yourself from External Influences to Attain Greatness

After having cleared steps 1 and 2, we are now focusing our discussion on the practical applications to attain greatness and are also comprehending how to seek the aid of the combination of our powerful minds and Nature. In the discussion so far, we have apprehended how to rouse the creativity lying inert within ourselves. In this context, you must also grasp that although creativity pours forth from many people, not every spark of creativity is as remarkable as that of Michael Jackson's, Picasso's or Charlie Chaplin's. Do you know why? Because even after one's creativity is kindled, the greater majority of people end up committing a grave mistake. To cite an example, writers generally read the works of a few great writers to gauge the tone, structure or various possible approaches to be used while writing. But this is exactly where they go astray, because then the influence of the writers they have read begins reflecting in their own writing, thereby dousing the spark of their originality. The creativity which had to be pure and original, which ought to have been inspired by one's inner self, is overshadowed by external influences. And in this process, they lose out on the beautiful and distinctive opportunity they had been granted. But then, this is not a singular trait of any one human being; everybody, right from painters, musicians, singers, writers to businessmen commit this grave mistake. To cite another example, if a musician listens to the tunes composed by other musicians excessively, it is bound to influence his own melodies. His originality will, thus, be lost in the labyrinths of mediocrity, and such being the case, great music will certainly never flow from him, because great creativity can spring forth only when one is free of all external influences. Let me state here that whatever I say is from my own personal experience; I have conducted workshops and lectures of over five hundred hours and in each one of them, I have covered new and unique topics. Indeed, never once have I repeated any topic in these five hundred hours. I am engaged in the continuous process of penning books, and I will perhaps, during the course of my entire life, write over a hundred books. You may well ask, how am I able to manage this? Well, my answer to your query is simple; in my entire life, neither have I listened to nor read anything in particular on the subject I write about. During my childhood, all that I had read were the works of Kabir, Lao Tzu and the

Bhagavad Gita...that is all! And this is precisely why, whenever I write or speak, all my observations are original and my language is also radically different from that of the others thronging the milieu. Thus, you must comprehend that the emergence of creativity from one's inner self is certainly noteworthy, but for such creativity to be termed great is an altogether different achievement. And if you want great creativity to issue from within you, then you must safeguard yourself from other creative influences pertaining to that field. Admittedly, scientists have to read up on the latest discoveries in their field and keep abreast of all information, but their ultimate goal is to eventually advance beyond that point and make new discoveries. Their only objective in reading about earlier discoveries is to make further progress in that subject. Hence, it can be said that fields associated with science are the only exception to this rule. In all other fields, each and every kind of external influence is nothing but an impediment to great creativity streaming forth from within. Having said that, there is nothing wrong in listening to or reading the works of other great people in the initial stage, but one must shield oneself from becoming unduly influenced; never allow such reading to make an imprint on one's own creativity. And, once creativity starts to flow from within, one should simply let go of everything else and let it continually flow. I'm sure those who have attained this stage would have fathomed the gravity of my words. As for the rest of the people, an allusion has verily been made for them, so I am certain that this point must be completely clear to them as well. Ergo, pass a resolution to ensure that the creativity emanating from within you shall (always) be great in nature. This resolution will safeguard you from other people's influences and ensure that every creativity emanating from you is original in nature.

Your Resolution

....

....

....

....

....

....

....

....

4. Embrace the Mercurial Nature of Creativity

As stated earlier, all kinds of creativity are a gift from Nature; the sparks of creativity are triggered in your inner minds by Nature, and all you have to endeavour is to let it pour forth. This is the only process through which all kinds of great creativity emerge. Ergo, you have no recourse save for accepting Nature's refuge in order to let any kind of great creativity emanate from within. For, creativity will pour forth only as per Nature's will and time, and it will emerge only in the manner it desires. Your role is simply confined to letting it stream from within you. If you try to do anything above and beyond this, then great creativity will never be able to spring forth from you. Thus, as far as creativity is concerned, never commit the folly of presuming, 'I will undertake such and such task tomorrow.' That is because, ultimately, creativity will only flow when Nature bestows it upon you, but if it holds back, then there is very little you can do about it. Hence, simply refrain from doing anything; do not try to force it out in any way. Else, 'you' will end up forcing your way in this process, and I have already explained that you have absolutely no role to play in the emergence of creativity. However, if you try to forcibly make creativity emanate from you, the outcome borne out of such creativity is bound to be worthless. That is precisely the reason why, I have reiterated that the only goal of step 3 is to elevate you to greatness. And lending greatness to man is a task meant for the combined powers of man's powerful minds and Nature; your role in this entire play is negligent, almost next to nothing. Hence, the entire science of step 3 revolves around surrendering yourself to Nature, and devoting yourself to its will.

In a nutshell, comprehend once and for all that great creativity will flow only as per Nature's will, at the precise time and in the manner it is ordained. Hence, never try to force yourself to 'do' anything creative; instead, always allow creativity to simply flow. Wait for Nature to send creativity to you; do not try to pry it out, otherwise you will end up ruining everything. There are a great many people who have waited for months together for creativity to flow forth, and as you know very well, good things come to those who wait. Ergo, great creativity has emanated only from those who have had patience, whereas those who have stubbornly tried to force creativity out have verily massacred their own creativity. I believe you must have grasped this simple point; so, without further ado, pass a firm resolution that will teach you how to wait, and help you refrain from doing anything creative by force. Indeed, those who are already creative must have taken this point to heart, because they must have committed this mistake several times in the past. But today, they must have, undoubtedly, learnt about the magic behind creativity; they must have discerned that Nature has the sole right over all kinds of creativity. With this point, I have made my allusion clear to everybody. Simply comprehend that this method will prove useful in all your endeavours. Thus, whenever you are undertaking a great task, step back and let Nature be at the forefront; let it take command over the creativity that will stem forth from you. Indubitably, if Nature performs the task instead of you, it will automatically become great, and the day you learn to entrust every task of yours to Nature, a miracle of the most profound nature will occur. Indeed, your endeavour of reading this book will become worthwhile. That being said, kindly compose a *Japa Mantra,* which will remind you to exercise patience and wait for creativity to burst forth.

Your *Japa Mantra*

....

....

....

....

....

....

....

....

....

5. Creativity is a Flow

As explained earlier, Nature has the sole right over every kind of creativity. It is Nature that sends a push of creativity, which then flows forth from your powerful minds. This is verily the fundamental principle pertaining to each and every kind of creativity. And when creativity is bestowed upon you in the form of a push, it implies that creativity is a flow, having a seamless movement. Flow implies that there is no hitch or jerk in terms of thinking or analysing at any point; creativity is sent by Nature and flows uninterruptedly through the mind. Thus, as far as creativity is concerned, know that there is no scope for thinking or deliberating, as everything occurs in a seamless flow. Great creativity can never stem forth by indulging in thinking or analysing, and perchance, if you are compelled to think and analyse when involved in some creative process, then know that you are still distanced from Nature. If you ever find yourself caught in this trap, instead of wasting your energy in considerable thought and analysis, take a pause and wait patiently till the time your minds are in complete alignment with Nature. But you must undertake any task only when you experience a push for that task from within. This law fits like a glove on poets, authors, writers, painters and musicians. And in the case of singers, actors and sportspeople, who have to continually practise, they too are required to give a spontaneous performance. In other words, at the time of performance, they also have to rely on flow, and if the flow does not emerge from within at the requisite moment, then even the greatest of sportspersons and performers fumble and fall flat. That is to say, their performance is also reliant on their connectivity with Nature. And when we speak of entrepreneurs and industrialists, although they are fully engaged in the initial process of thinking and analysing, the final decision is always based on their intuition, which emanates from within, thus, helping them make spontaneous decisions. And, remember the irrefutable truth that only those who make the final decision spontaneously succeed in becoming great businessmen and industrialists. Verily, every great industrialist and businessman's life bears testimony to this fact.

In short, all I want to impress upon you is that only the person whose mind is in complete alignment with Nature can well comprehend the meaning of spontaneity and flow, and as for the rest, they would be at sea trying to grasp the very fact of how great tasks occur without any thought or effort. However, you must focus on the fact that all the great feats of the world are obliged to the flow sent from Nature, where man has simply not meddled with this flow; and through this book, we are trying to learn exactly how to not meddle with this flow. For, without knowing this, nothing great will ever occur. And 'thinking and making an effort' is nothing but intervening in this flow. For instance, scientists, in order to make new inventions or discoveries, have to engage in thinking to prepare the initial groundwork, but once they become completely immersed in their experiment, the grand breakthrough verily occurs in a flow. The point I want to drive home is, all scientific miracles are also beholden only to Nature's flow.

On this note, you must also comprehend that every flow sent through Nature is marked by a unique perfection. As I have stated earlier, authors, writers, poets, thinkers, painters, musicians and so on have to depend on this flow for creativity, and every flow that surges forth from them is the ultimate height of perfection. Whether it is Krishna's Gita, Kabir's couplets or Khalil Gibran's compositions, everything is obliged to Nature's flow. That is why, those who are wise do not say that Krishna composed the Gita or Kabir uttered the couplets. They say, Gita flowed through Krishna's consciousness and the couplets flowed from Kabir's. And flowing implies that there can be no mistake of even a comma or a full stop in that which has flown. Krishna is not finding faults in what has been uttered through him. There is no need to find faults in it either. For, nothing can be more perfect than spontaneity.

I hope, after this detailed discussion, you must have fathomed every nitty-gritty regarding creativity and must have also apprehended that creativity (of any kind) surges forth in a spontaneous flow through Nature. The next point you need to grasp is, although millions of people engage in creative pursuits, only a handful of them attain greatness. Why is this so? It is simply because the majority of people try their hands at a creative task only after mulling deeply over it and spending considerable time deliberating upon it; if I were to state this in simple terms, they try to wrest creativity out of themselves in a forceful manner. But know this for a fact that such an approach will never result in anything even remotely great, because great creativity is nothing but a flow, which pours forth from within. Thus, if you truly wish to attain greatness, minimise thinking and analysing when engaging in creative pursuits; it would, indeed, serve you well if you wait for creativity to flow naturally. And eventually, this wait will itself establish your connection with Nature. Albeit, I am well aware, to instil this quality of patience is a well-nigh difficult proposition, therefore, to smoothen the path, I will suggest a method. It is simple really, all that you have to do is continue to muse on creativity deep within yourself, in the solitude of your being. Become completely immersed in it; make no attempts except waiting patiently for creativity to gush forth from within. Initially, the progress may be slow, but a day will dawn when the flow will come pouring forth in a torrent from within... And when it comes, you will be left dumbstruck. It will care neither for night nor day, but simply gush out from you; and this is, indeed, an invaluable experience. It is my ardent wish that everybody should experience such a surge of creativity one day. Interestingly, when the flow gushes forth, many months' worth of work will get accomplished in a matter of hours and that too with absolute perfection. And at that time, in that moment of realisation, you will comprehend in entirety that creativity is not your slave to flow as per your time and convenience, as per your whims and desires; its push will verily come from within only when Nature wills. That is precisely why, those who are creative are never able to perform as per your demand, because they are reliant on that elusive flow for performance. This is one of the reasons why creative people are generally deemed as very moody. But comprehend once and for all that they are not moody; rather they are dependent upon Nature's flow. With this elucidation, I hope you must have comprehended this profound point of spiritual science.

Now, apprehend another key point with respect to creativity; it is not necessary that all the creativity will pour forth in one single instance. Many a time, creativity comes forth in spurts. Thus, when creativity flows from you, pick up your pen or brush and create a perfect piece of art in harmony with Nature, and then rest awhile. After some time has elapsed, you will be nudged again and experience another push of creativity; when this feeling is kindled, know for sure that this is a signal to resume work once again. Know that all great works, whether it is literature, music or art, have come into existence in this manner alone. There is just one principle of creativity; no matter the amount of creativity that comes forth or when it surges, it will always come in a flow and be spontaneous. However, it is not necessary for all of it to flow in one instance.

Hence, if you wish to do something great, pass a steadfast resolution to that effect without further ado. Resolve that, 'As far as possible, I will not force creativity upon myself by thinking about it or making an effort to wrest it out in any way; rather I will muse over that creativity in solitude and wait for it to flow seamlessly. Come what may, I will rest only once I have established a connection between my powerful minds and Nature. I will surely experience this great *leela*, this great play of Nature.' In this way, compose a *Japa Mantra* for yourself in your own words, and then continually ruminate over it. This will help you connect with Nature. Simply resolve that you will not rest until you establish a connection with Nature. And once Nature grabs your hand, miraculous wonders will suffuse your life with their many-splendoured hues.

Your *Japa Mantra*

....

....

....

....

....

....

....

....

Now that you have passed a firm resolution, comprehend one final point in this context. The entire game of attaining greatness hinges upon when you stop 'doing', because the only point which you need to imbibe in step 3 is, nothing shall materialise by your 'doing'. You will have to realise that elevating man to greatness is a task that is dependent on the tuning between man's powerful minds and Nature. Only if you leave everything to them, will you be able to become great and that is precisely what we are discussing in step 3. In short, in step 3, the practical applications will teach you how to entrust everything in your life to your powerful minds and Nature. Now, comprehend that once man becomes great, an enormous amount of wealth, glory, respect and honour invariably showers upon his life. But, tell me, what did man really do to this end? Well, he did nothing save for establishing a tuning between his powerful minds and Nature. And when he has done absolutely nothing, there is no question of him becoming vain and arrogant either. This is verily the reason why you must have always found people like Bill Gates, Ratan Tata, Stephen Hawking and others of their ilk to be very simple and humble, and this is what exalts their position to even greater heights of greatness. Thus, be cautious and safeguard yourself from conceit and pride over every small success, for, the moment these emotions lace your thinking and actions, they will throttle the very creativity flowing from you. Embed this firmly in your mind, arrogance implies 'you' as an individual, and there is absolutely no chance of any bonding developing between 'you' and Nature. Nature works for the greater good, and there is no chance that it will favour you individually. I hope you will remember this significant point on your journey to attaining greatness. Success should humble you and the more success you attain, the humbler and simpler you should become...and one day, this simplicity and humility will verily lend you greatness. Do not break the flow of Nature's creativity by getting entangled in petty arrogance, else you will be deprived of achieving greatness. Therefore, all creative people must remember to safeguard themselves from arrogance.

The Burden of the Entire World is Not Thrust Upon You

Each body is wounded, every soul is parched...
All eyes are troubled, and every heart is desolate...
Is this the world or the kingdom of senselessness?

This Urdu couplet penned by the great poet Sahir Ludhianvi gives an apt picture of the state the world is in, wherein every person is either weary or worried, engulfed in a dark cloud of misery and disquiet, or embroiled in some or the other struggle. The moot question is, why is the world languishing in this deplorable state? Who is responsible for it? Well, the answer is, man is himself responsible for his sorry state. Because every person lives his life overwhelmed by the belief that the enormous weight of setting his life on the path of progress has been dumped upon his shoulders. And he has no recourse but to move heaven and earth in order to make that happen... and then, he gets caught up in the rat race. And not just one race but a multitude of races! He desires to be religious as well as social, he yearns to be educated as well as knowledgeable, and above all, he wishes to conquer the world, because he is weighed down by the enormous task of setting his life.

This begs the question, why doesn't anybody take a moment to ponder and rove an eye over Nature? Why don't you stop and notice that there is someone who wields the baton and takes care of everything, right from managing the entire universe with its mighty moon and the stars to this very Earth. There is someone who is making the rivers flow and the winds blow. This being the case, Nature's power is indubitably far greater than our scope of thinking and imagination. And when all of this stands true, there is but one question which we must ask ourselves; would not the one who is governing everything, be governing our lives as well? Why, of course, it is so and the goal of step 3 is to surrender to that ultimate power. Frankly speaking, only a person who surrenders to the sole authority of the universe i.e. to Nature, can be termed religious in the truest sense of the word. Do not commit the mistake of considering the so-called community leaders as religious, because that is also an extension of the web of ignorance that has blinded everyone. And besides, how can someone who runs behind communities be called great? It is the easiest course to choose, for, it strengthens the ego, and that is precisely why, the entire world is entangled in the web of communities. Unfortunately, they have also warped everyone's minds by instilling in them the absurd pride of superiority—the belief that one's own community is better than the others. And as this false pride appeals to an ordinary human being, he concurs with this ideology. However, the sad truth is, most of these people are still desolate and defeated. Trials and struggles continue to torment such people, and with each passing day, they continue to be further mired in them. Unfortunately, there is no chance of them getting rid of their problems either, for, life can be set on the path of progress only by becoming truly religious, and a truly religious person is someone who has renounced his 'ego', who does not nurse the erroneous belief that an enormous weight of setting his life has been dumped on his shoulders. A true theist is one who entrusts the reins of his life to Nature, who surrenders to Nature completely. And this is, indeed, easier said than done. If truth be told, there is a veritable dearth of knowledge on this subject as well. But I hope you have realised that one cannot attain greatness without Nature's support, for, the flow of creativity from within is the prerequisite to attain any kind of greatness. And Nature has the sole authority over every kind of creativity. In the initial part of step 3, we also grasped how to procure Nature's assistance to that end. And I am sanguine that everybody must have thoroughly imbibed this ultimate principle of spiritual science.

This raises the question, why does every human being falter, despite employing all means and methods to progress? It is simply because nobody apprehends their own ultimate authority; actually, every human being in this world undermines his own strengths, but the truth is, he is far more powerful than what he considers himself to be. The only law he needs to be mindful of is, he should not wage life's battle alone; rather he should make allies of his powerful minds and Nature. This single act on his part will overnight bequeath him with powers that are thousand times more powerful than what he presently possesses. And steps 1 and 2 are the processes that enable him to become powerful, whereas step 3 is the ultimate explosion of power. Because in this step, you have been provided with a few practical applications that will help you garner assistance from your powerful minds and Nature. So far, we have comprehended how to derive assistance from your powerful minds and Nature for creativity to flow forth. In the subsequent part of the book, we will discuss how to garner their assistance in order to make the key decisions of life, and also how to tackle the principal problems of life with their support. For, there are verily impediments and roadblocks in the path of attaining greatness as well. Even great people have to live in this world whilst enduring the ebbs and flows that are a part and parcel of life; highs and lows are an inevitable part of life as per the irrefutable law of life. However, these problems can be dealt with if the right solutions are used to tackle them. So now, I will straightaway provide a few practical applications to solve the key problems of your life with the assistance of 'the tuning between your powerful minds and Nature'. At the same time, I will also provide you some applications which will help you comprehend how to make life's key decisions. Just remember that your powerful minds and Nature are far more powerful and aware than your knowledge and ego. Ergo, without their cooperation, neither will you be able to attain greatness, nor will you be able to dispel problems from your life. So, without further ado, let us proceed to those practical applications.

Applications for Making Life's Key Decisions

1. Discern Truth-Untruth in a Moment

Man wishes to comprehend and garner knowledge about a great many things so that he can arrive at the right decision in every matter. Now, as far as the day-to-day decisions of life are concerned, this makes sense because having knowledge proves handy while making such decisions. For example, decisions pertaining to what sort of clothes to wear, which restaurant to choose for dining, what items to purchase or where to go on a holiday. However, for making all significant decisions beyond this point, your knowledge and comprehension prove to be of no use. Although your knowledge and understanding prove effective in making small and insignificant decisions, it cannot discern truth and lies. For that purpose, you will verily have to accept the refuge of your Spontaneous Mind, which is adept at discerning every truth and lie, and I will show you the method of utilising it to your benefit. For instance, if you contract pain in your chest, you will naturally rush to consult a doctor. Now, your chest pain could be attributed to indigestion or it could even signify some ailment of the heart. If the doctor is honest, he will conduct a proper analysis and tell you rightly what you are suffering from. But not all doctors are honest; there have been innumerable instances wherein the doctor has conducted a heart surgery and handed a hefty bill to the patient despite him suffering only from indigestion. Now, in such cases, how does one decide whether the doctor is speaking the truth or spouting lies? So, for that purpose, simply apprise the doctor of your problem and step aside. Then, let whatever the doctor says enter your mind; let it seep directly to your Spontaneous Mind. Do not mull over or analyse whatever he is saying. Do not let your knowledge or analysis or even your fear come into the picture. Do not think even for a moment that this is your problem. Let the doctor's prognosis percolate deep inside you, just the way it is. If it goes within you in its pure form, then your Spontaneous Mind will let you know in a moment the extent of truth or lies in the doctor's words. You will know whether he has even comprehended your problem or not. And this answer will always be apt; it will never mislead you. Furthermore, you will simultaneously discern the nature of your real problem by the doctor's manner of speaking and the seriousness in his tone. This is verily that impressive feat of your Spontaneous Mind, which you must definitely know how to employ.

To summarise this segment, this is your internal mechanism of discerning truth and lies, and I have showed you the method of employing it too. Regardless of what a person is saying, if you let their words enter straight within, without becoming a party to it, then the correct answer of whether the person is speaking the truth or is blatantly lying will be revealed to you from within. You will comprehend everything in the snap of a finger if you let the words enter within, without letting your knowledge or analysis interfere. However, a person who has not passed steps 1 and 2 will simply not be able to extricate himself from this equation; he will fail to comprehend that his intelligence and knowledge are limited, whereas Nature is boundless. Why, Nature is the supreme power which is even cognisant of what is going on within everyone and this very Nature is connected with your Spontaneous Mind. So, accept its refuge and withdraw yourself to gauge the truth. And in order to do that, pass a firm resolution to this effect. Write down in your own words, 'I have employed my intelligence endlessly and brandished a great deal of knowledge, but despite this, the majority of my decisions have gone wrong. Henceforth, I will not interfere at all. I must not allow my vain knowledge to interfere in this process. I must stop worrying about myself and hand over the reins of all my decisions to my Spontaneous Mind. No matter what someone says, I have to let the information reach straight to my Spontaneous Mind.' Pass a firm resolution along these lines in your own words. And whenever you are on the verge of making any important decision, recite it like a *Japa Mantra*. Furthermore, start adopting this *Japa Mantra* even for making the small, day-to-day decisions of life. Entrust your worry to that power, which has brought you into existence, and believe me, you will triumph in every sphere of life.

Your *Japa Mantra*

....

....

....

....

....

....

2. Entrust Life's Key Decisions to Nature

We all have to make certain momentous decisions in our lives. If all those decisions taken by us prove to be right, our life verily turns into a wonderful and memorable journey. And all those decisions, right from which career path to opt for to choosing your life partner fall under the category of key decisions. Whichever field one may be employed in, one verily has to take decisions; in business one has to decide whether it is feasible to start a factory or not, or whom to enter into partnership with. It is a given that while making all such decisions, a human being verily thinks of his best interests, and he makes all calculations to that end as well. However, despite this, most of the decisions of the majority of people still prove wrong, and consequently, their life fails to become as beautiful and wondrous as they desire it to be. So, what must one do in such a scenario? How must one arrive at the right decision? There is but one solution to it—surrender yourself and accept Nature's refuge. As long as you allow your thinking, analysis and calculations to intervene, all your decisions will continually misfire. Take for instance, the decision of entering into matrimony. Man considers all possible factors when arriving at this decision. He accords lengthy consideration to every aspect, pondering at length about the prospective bride or groom, right from their education, nature, family, religion to even social standing. And if this were not enough, he even solicits the opinions of a great number of people; he adjusts the timing of his matrimony to align with the placement of the moon and the stars and even matches the horoscopes! Furthermore, he solemnises the marriage as per religious principles and rituals; but despite this, the majority of marriages stumble down the rickety path, eventually becoming a pain in the neck. Do you know why this is so? Because a great deal of thinking, deliberating and so-called knowledge has gone into this decision, while Nature's will has not been sought at all. In other words, a crucial decision as this does not call for thinking and deliberating; Nature's consent alone suffices. If one ties the knot taking into account Nature's blessing, not only will the married couple always enjoy marital bliss, but they will also prove instrumental in each other's progress.

This begets the question, how does one ascertain Nature's will? There is but one solution: withdraw yourself and your knowledge from the equation. When you meet the prospective bride, keep your head clear of all thoughts. Do not spare a single thought to her education, religion, caste-creed and family. After all, you are marrying the girl, not her caste or her family. So, just look at the girl calmly, and then let that matter completely slip away from your mind. In fact, do not even ask for other people's opinion because it is you, who will marry her, not them. That being said, it is quite possible that the answer might not come at once, because after all, this is not an everyday decision, but one of the few crucial decisions of life. Hence, it is obvious that these decisions will take time, because they will first be scrutinised in Nature's court, and only then will the decisions manifest eventually. Ergo, allow some time for this decision to manifest; during this interval, carry on with your normal routine without giving the matter any thought. After a few days elapse, you will get a specific answer either in affirmation or against it. Simply follow it through, and there will be absolutely no hitch. Let me tell you, the people who have married as per the decision declared by Nature have proven to be matches made in heaven. Indeed, all those who have taken decisions in this manner are verily providing testimony to this fact by leading a glorious life, while on the other hand, countless troubled marriages are also present before our eyes as a proof of decisions based on intense thinking, calculations and deliberations.

That being said, bear in mind that only a person who has vanquished his ego will receive complete assistance from his powerful minds and Nature. But first, comprehend what ego implies. Ego is nurturing the belief that I am wise and intelligent. I am so knowledgeable that I am capable of making all my decisions by myself. Whoever upholds this erroneous presumption will be left bereft of Nature's assistance; and comprehend clearly that it is not easy at all to forsake such a presumption. Not everyone is capable of living their lives without worrying about themselves, and that is precisely why, not everyone can become great. Ergo, wipe out your existence. Kindle the understanding that...'I know nothing; nobody save for Nature is wise.' Only then will these solutions prove effective. All those who are great are already cognisant of all these tricks, and you can also elevate yourself to greatness with the assistance of Nature, by wiping out every trace of your existence. And when greatness is verily within your grasp, what are you waiting for? Go ahead and embrace it! I am handing over the ultimate weapon of spiritual science to you, so derive the utmost benefit from it. Having read all the above-mentioned points, make a steadfast resolution in your own words to this end. Then, whenever you find yourself standing at a crossroads in life and need to take a vital decision, take recourse of this *Japa Mantra* penned by yourself and prepare to make an apt decision. Simply grasp that the answer emerging from within, in the form of yes or no, is what is known as intuition, and intuition is the language of Nature. All your decisions can prove wrong, but the intuition of a person who lives entrusting his life completely to Nature can never be wrong. So, without further ado, prepare yourself for this great achievement.

....

....

....

....

....

....

....

3. Undertake Tasks Only With Mind's Agreement

What a ludicrous situation man is entrapped in! A thousand and one tasks are supposed to be undertaken in the span of a single lifetime; and in doing so, man has truly turned himself into a machine, led astray by his own thinking. The majority of people find several tasks equally important and worth accomplishing in a single day. Now, in the span of a day, man can work for eight, ten or at the most, twelve hours, and with that, the day is surely going to draw to a close. Simply stated, while time has its own boundary, the list of tasks is boundless. Besides, in today's age, even a student has an endless to-do list; he must study, attend school and coaching class, complete his homework, play, watch cartoons, spend time with his friends and also fulfil the wishes of his parents. In other words, even the student of today's contemporary age has been reduced to the pathetic state of having to complete a hundred tasks during the span of a single day. In such a case, it is best not to enquire about an employed person, who behaves as if every second of his day is as precious as gold! And despite being so busy, running around in trying to complete all his tasks, when he closes his eyes at night, he lets out a deep sigh, and with a heavy heart, ponders over the many tasks that were left unfinished. Ironically, despite spending every living moment from the cradle to the grave in a state of busyness, man is not able to achieve any remarkable feat in life; instead, his life fritters away in sorrows, troubles and endless strife and struggles.

But why is this the case? There is only one plausible answer; this is the outcome of your own thinking and deliberation. You have been reduced to this pathetic state owing to your own futile knowledge and nonsensical attractions. Due to this, the list of seemingly crucial tasks became increasingly longer and eventually, they all proved worthless. Consequently, life frittered away in working oneself to the bone, and yet, there was nothing noteworthy that you could accomplish. Now, if you wish to safeguard yourself from this deleterious outcome, there is only one recourse at your disposal, and that is surrendering yourself to Nature. Having said that, what does surrendering oneself to Nature imply? It implies that the tasks to be undertaken and even the amount of tasks to be undertaken must be determined by one's co-ordination and connection with Nature. As mentioned earlier, Nature is connected with your powerful minds. Ergo, let the decision of whether a task has to be accomplished or not, be determined only by their connection. Set aside your perception and needs, and undertake only those tasks for which the mind is 100 percent in agreement. Engage yourself in only those many tasks, and accomplish them only when the mind is ready to be immersed in them completely. That is to say, your judgement of whether a task is urgent or important holds no meaning; your undertaking of that task would be fruitful only if your mind also considers it to be so. If your mind itself is not ready to perform any task, but you still insist on undertaking it, then you are acting against Nature's wishes, and let me tell you, the greater majority of people are performing most of their tasks contrary to Nature's wishes. They are engaging in those tasks only because they consider them important and advantageous. But such thinking on your part is fallacious; Nature has no part to play in this; indeed, this is the very reason why, the tasks which are undertaken listlessly and dispiritingly do not bring exemplary results. This is precisely why, even though everybody is engaged in performing a great many tasks, the results accruing from them are almost negligent.

I am certain, the question you are tempted to ask is, 'In what manner must one undertake tasks so that they can engender fruitful results?' My dear reader, it is only to apprise you of the same that I am laying down all these foundations. Think of it in this way; everybody in this world wants to set their life on the path of progress, and everybody is also aware that they would have to undertake a number of tasks to achieve that goal. The train of thought up to this point is well on track, but the problem arises thereafter, because everyone becomes confused as to when they must undertake tasks and which tasks to undertake. The majority of human beings, lured by external attractions and succumbing to pressure, compose an unending list of tasks. But in doing so, they themselves get confused about which task to accord first priority to and which tasks to defer? Their situation turns even more precarious, for, in this state of confusion, they are unable to concentrate on any of their present tasks; and this, unfortunately, is the sorry state of almost every human being. There is just one solution to safeguard yourself from this trap, and that is to accept complete refuge of your powerful minds, because they are well connected with Nature, and Nature knows better than you what is in your best interests. Thus, perform only those tasks for which you have Nature's blessing. At the same time, engage in those tasks only when Nature nudges you to undertake them. Now, you might ask, how will we come to know if Nature wants us to undertake a particular task? Alright, so let me guide you...it is extremely simple...all you have to do is, relinquish your thoughts, needs, attractions and pressures. Grasp once and for all that these distractions are only leading you astray. As soon as you adopt this stance, your entire life will undergo a sea change; the once busy and overwrought person who was running helter-skelter to accomplish a great number of tasks will now find ample time on his hands. For, nothing is urgent or important anymore, and all that remains is a lengthy list of tasks to do, so let that list be. If you have surrendered yourself to Nature, then let Nature send you a sign. Remember, faith and patience is the absolute criterion one must meet in order to attain any blessing of Nature, and unfortunately, everybody finds themselves unable to fulfil this very condition. Not everyone is capable of sitting in peace with a carefree attitude and entrusting their worries to

Nature, and that is precisely why, not everyone is capable of attaining greatness either.

I can well gauge the next question you are eager to ask, which is, 'What will happen, now that we have eschewed all our urgency and sat down in repose?' So, let me tell you, once you have succeeded in accomplishing this feat, consider your work almost done. Then, after a short wait, your mind will become hundred percent interested in undertaking any one particular task, and when this occurs, that task will be accomplished by you automatically. Once that task has been dealt with, there will again come a period of rest and this resting period can range from hours to days, and in the case of momentous tasks, even up to months. In other words, this period of repose can stretch to a few hours or days for small tasks and up to months where momentous tasks are concerned. So, let it extend for as long as it does, you simply entrust all your worries to Nature's ultimate authority and wait patiently for the next sign from Nature. Post every resting period, you will once again receive a hundred percent push from Nature to undertake a fresh task; it is only then that you will deal with that task. But a word to the wise, do not dwell over the gain or loss that will ensue thereafter; perform any task only at the behest of Nature and leave its outcome solely upon Nature. Your job is simply to swing between the moments of rest and the periods of activity, wherein you perform tasks with hundred percent absorption of the mind. You cannot even begin to imagine the great heights of success you will achieve with this one change, and that too, without suffering any kind of hardship and without stifling your mind. All great people have attained greatness simply by treading this very path. That is why, let me reiterate, your life will be steered on the path of progress by surrendering yourself to Nature, not by heeding to arrogance; and this is verily the ultimate principle of Nature.

On this note, let us comprehend the entire math behind the design of Nature. Man is not unsuccessful because he shirks work; rather, success eludes him because he undertakes a multitude of pointless tasks, sometimes lured by attractions and yielding to pressures, while at other times, compelled by his thoughts and needs. But the entire game of human life hinges upon only a handful of important tasks, and it is Nature that determines those tasks for every human being. Furthermore, your mind also becomes hundred percent ready and willing to perform those tasks which are determined by Nature, and only those many tasks are really in your best interests. Thus, as far as possible, stop engaging in tasks in which your heart shows scant interest, and by doing so, half the problems that you are stricken with will be resolved in no time. Then, spend the time you have saved—which is nothing but a period of rest between two tasks—to relax majestically, and experience for yourself how the remainder of your problems also dissipate. Why do you not comprehend that you are a human being, not a machine; you cannot perform tasks one after the other mechanically without stopping; rest and relaxation are as vital in your life as the accomplishment of significant tasks. You have mired yourself in busyness and the hustle and bustle only because of your failure to comprehend this point; as a result, you have turned into a zombie leading a mechanical life, instead of revelling in the pleasures of the grand life that a human being is wont to live. In fact, you have now busied yourself to such an extent that you are busier than the greatest of industrialists! Why, even Bill Gates and Mark Zuckerberg do not have as many crucial tasks to undertake as you do! Indeed, all that I want to impress upon you is, you must undertake any task only when your mind is hundred percent ready and inclined to perform that task, because this state of mind—of becoming hundred percent ready—is verily a sign from Nature's end. And after every task is undertaken, there invariably comes a period of rest, and this interval of repose is also equally important. During this interval, you should replenish yourself with fresh energy and vigour; you should spend this period of leisure the way you wish to, pandering to your heart's desires. Thereafter, you will feel energised once again to undertake a new task with hundred percent willingness and absorption. I assure you, you will yourself be surprised to see the strides you make as a result of this process.

Let me now try to explain this point citing the example of students. Children in today's world are embroiled in one task or the other for almost ten hours daily, busy as they are with studies, school, tuition and homework. Can you tell me, what is the objective behind this extent of busyness, all year long? Only to comprehend a thousand or two thousand odd pages? Now, a youthful mind has a number of fancies of its own, which it is wont to fulfil, but they all get suppressed under the pressure of studies. That is the reason why, a student finds himself unable to fully concentrate on his studies, and consequently, while he toils and labours his utmost, he passes with mediocre grades. Now, what is the task that children are entrusted with? Only to study a thousand or two thousand odd pages all through the year, and present them during the exams in a manner that will fetch them good grades, right? So, when the task is so trivial, it will happen on its own; just leave it to Nature. If your mind is not hundred percent invested in it, do not study; consider it as a period of rest and indulge in the fancies of your youthful mind. There is no need for you to spend long, anxious hours fretting over not being able to memorise your lesson; instead, leave all your study woes in the hands of Nature and let it take care of it. After every period of rest, Nature invariably makes your mind abound with hundred percent interest in studies. So, sit with your books when your mind is hundred percent ready to be immersed in that task, and then see the remarkable feat it achieves; surely, you will be left dazed at the results! In just a week of studying, you will accomplish that which other students are unable to accomplish even after toiling throughout the month, with their heads buried in the books. And perhaps, you will learn several other things too in the time that you ended up saving. You must have heard that Swami Vivekananda used to read a thousand pages in an hour, and then he would also retell the same, verbatim. He was able to achieve this marvellous feat, because whenever he undertook a task, he executed it as per Nature's will, with hundred percent willingness of his mind. On this note, tell me, what sets life on the path of progress? Certainly, superlative performance. And when is such a performance possible? Only when the mind is completely absorbed in the task at hand. And mind you, you cannot make your mind become absorbed in anything, as and when you wish. Your mind does not become absorbed in any task just because you think it is beneficial or necessary. On the contrary, one's mind becomes absorbed in a task only if Nature wills it, and eventually, only those (many) tasks prove to be fruitful. To re-emphasise what I have discussed so far, whichever way you may choose to perceive it, you will never prosper and progress in life without entrusting all your worries to Nature.

On my part, I am expounding the most profound spiritual science to you, but you will be able to comprehend this remarkable science only when you have gained a few experiences of it yourself. All these matters cannot be comprehended without experiencing them. To cite a simple example, can a person who has never eaten a piece of sweet all his life ever experience what sweetness is, regardless of the many descriptions you provide him with? To savour the saccharine taste and experience it, it is imperative that he should have eaten something sweet at least once in his life. Now, the experience I am referring to is far beyond the experience of discovering what sweetness is. Thus, you simply cannot apprehend it without experiencing it yourself; however, those who are great, those who are creative... will grasp this concept in an instant, because they have had experiences of the same. To summarise, you need to grasp the concept of undertaking any task with hundred percent absorption of mind, and then relaxing sincerely and wholeheartedly. Once you have firmly ensconced yourself into this process, this entire system will automatically fall into place in a seamless manner, and then, Nature itself will get all important tasks accomplished through you. For, you have now verily become Nature's 'instrument'. On this note, let me cite the example of Edison to elucidate this point further. As popularly known, Edison had registered more than a thousand patents to his name. Now, do you think he dove into a fresh experiment as soon as he finished the previous one? Certainly not...! There invariably came a period of rest between two experiments, and he got more than a thousand patents registered to his name following this very procedure. On the other hand, if one were to follow the education system of today, an entire lifetime would prove insufficient just to fathom a thousand patents! Forget inventing something new, even comprehending an existing invention would turn into an onerous task.

I believe, you must have comprehended this point in entirety. So, without further ado, pass a firm resolution in your own words in order to put it into practice. Write in your resolution, 'I have comprehended that any task in which Nature's will is not involved can never prove to be productive. Thus, I hereby entrust all my concerns for setting my life on the path of progress to Nature. I will undertake only those tasks for which Nature makes my mind hundred percent ready, and I will wait patiently until it sends me a sign. But come what may, I will undertake a task only upon Nature's direction. I will not worry about anything over and beyond this.' Incorporate this in your own words and compose a *Japa Mantra* accordingly. And know well that this is an extremely potent *mantra*. Ergo, contemplate over it every morning and continue to do so till the time it becomes firmly embedded within you and you succeed in effortlessly putting it into practice.

Your *Japa Mantra*

....

....

....

....

....

....

....

....

Nevertheless, I am aware that to forsake worries about oneself is no easy task. Not everyone is capable of liberating themselves from external attractions and pressures, and besides, you have also muddled up your life by setting off on the wrong path. Consequently, whether your mind is inclined towards the task or not, or whether your heart is in it or not, a number of tasks indubitably seem crucial to you. Obviously, you cannot hold Nature or me accountable in this regard, because you have yourself chosen the wrong path in life. The one and only culprit for the mess you find yourself in is you, and that is why, at the initial stage, you will feel a certain amount of trepidation in veering from your existing path. A number of complications will rear their head, and you will be assailed with thoughts such as, 'If I do not undertake such and such task, I will be in grave trouble, and if I fail to perform such and such deed, my doom is guaranteed.' But it is natural to be assailed with such feelings, so relax and do not fret; initially, continue to deal with the small and petty tasks half-heartedly, but as far as the important decisions are concerned, it is best to wait for Nature's indication. Comprehend that all these complications exist because you have confined your life in parameters set by others, by setting off on the wrong path. Had you chosen the true and right path from the outset, you would have scaled great heights in life by now. Even so, it is never too late to start afresh. So, henceforth, endeavour to bury your past actions and march forth on the right path as much as possible.

4. Never Make a Decision When You're in a Dilemma

Oft-times in life, there are instances wherein you find yourself standing at a crossroads, unsure of which path to take, for, both look convincing enough to tread on. To cite an example, let's suppose that although you like the girl you are about to marry, you are unable to convince yourself completely to tie the knot with her. Or let's say that although a proposed business scheme seems attractive, you can't help but harbour some misgivings about it. You are invariably faced with numerous such situations in your life. So, what must one do in such instances? Well, simply accept Nature's refuge. Do not try to arrive at any decision by working out your own math or by making calculations that serve your self-interest. Don't be in a hurry to choose one of the two options. Truth be told, it is this haste and impetuosity, which has led to the ruin of humankind. Hence, do not force yourself to arrive at any decision. Know for certain that any decision you make in a dilemma will doubtless be a harbinger of trouble and hardship. After a few days, you are bound to rue, 'Alas! If only I had chosen the other option!' Thus, know this in no uncertain terms that Nature is vested with the knowledge of all three facets of time. It is fully aware and far better equipped than you to know what lies in your best interests. So, simply leave the decision to Nature. And how should you do that...? Well, simply entrust both options to the back of your mind and forget about them; engage yourself in some other activity. Then, one day, all of a sudden, a firm and clear decision will emerge from within, to choose either one of the options, and the other option will vanish on its own. Only one of the options between whether to get married or not will remain; all you need to do is simply follow it through. Know for certain that this decision of yours will be made hundred percent by your mind. And I have already stated, Nature's wish is verily contained in anything that transpires with the full complicity of the mind. Now that you have comprehended this subject so well, there is no need for me to delve into further detail. Thus, pass a firm resolution in your own words, on how to make a decision when you find yourself in a dilemma. Then, every time you are caught in a quandary, make this *mantra* your *Japa Mantra* and contemplate over it; this will prove helpful in entrusting that decision to Nature. Write in your resolution, 'I will place both options in my mind and leave them to Nature. Then, I will relinquish all thoughts regarding that matter and busy myself in other tasks. I will wait for a clear decision, either in the affirmative or otherwise, to come from Nature.' Just include all points covering these aspects in this resolution.

Your *Japa Mantra*

....

....

....

....

....

....

....

....

5. Choose One Task at a Time

Oft-times, we are met with unexpected situations wherein we are required to attend to a few urgent tasks simultaneously. To illustrate, let's suppose you have an important meeting at work, but the same day your father falls critically ill, and to make the situation even more strenuous, you are expecting guests at your house. Overwhelmed with a multitude of situations that seem equally important, you are caught in a dilemma of which task should be tackled first. Indeed, during such times, your mind struggles to arrive at a decision regarding which task should be accorded topmost priority. Many a time, your mind feels the urge to deal with everything at once. In other words, such situations make you utterly confused and perturbed. Thus, when you find yourself in the throes of such a situation, straightaway select one task. And make this choice neither by calculations based on your intelligence nor by thoughts of possible gain or loss... Select the task towards which your mind is most inclined, the one which your mind concurs with the most. Then, dive headlong into that task, and during the interim period, entrust the remaining tasks to Nature's system of justice. Do not think that the weight of your entire life has fallen on your shoulders. If several important tasks have cropped up at the same time, then choose one and leave the rest to Nature. Nature will undoubtedly assist you with your remaining tasks, but bear in mind that the rest of the tasks should slip away from your mind, and you should become completely immersed in your chosen task. Neither should you worry about the remaining tasks, nor should their thought even cross your mind. Then, Nature will verily take care of those tasks for you. Tell me, how difficult is it for the power which is managing the entire world to manage your life? Thus, all you have to do is learn to entrust your tasks to Nature. Because Nature will never worry about a task that you are already harbouring a worry for. Nature will worry about your remaining tasks only when you have entrusted those tasks absolutely to Nature, casting away all worries pertaining to them. Why is it so difficult for you to grasp the fact that you do not have to take care of all your life's tasks alone? It is an indelible truth that Nature verily is present to take care of the majority of crucial tasks of your life. And letting Nature deal with those tasks is, indeed, in your best interests. Thus, you will have to learn to entrust your tasks to Nature. But yes, if you finish the first task and you still have time and energy to spare, then deal with the second task as well. But focus on undertaking only one task at a time, and in the interim, entrust the other tasks to Nature. This is verily a magical solution that will make all of life's battles easier.

I believe, you must have thoroughly comprehended this point, which I have explained in brief. So, what are you waiting for? Pass a firm resolution to that end in your own words. And then, whenever several tasks crop up all at once, consider your resolution as a *Japa Mantra* and reflect on it constantly; meditate over it till the time you choose any one task to perform and entrust the rest to Nature. And then, behold the miracle that Nature works for you!

Your *Japa Mantra*

....

....

....

....

....

....

....

....

6. Liberate Yourself From Problems Instantly

Every person in the world is besieged by a multitude of problems. This demands introspection on our part and raises the question, is every person's life really teeming with so many problems? If truth be told, the preponderance of a human being's problems are imaginary and unrealistic; he himself creates them by continuously dwelling on them. And if you wish to lead a beautiful life, then you will simply have to break this habit. For, how can a person whose life is burdened by a plethora of problems ever be able to revel in the pleasures of life? Besides, how can human life be besieged with so many problems when Nature exists in all its power and glory? Such a situation need not arise at all, it is simply out of the question; hence, it follows that you must doubtless be making some mistake yourself. So, just rectify that mistake and eliminate your problems today itself, from this very moment.

I am well aware that you will raise the question, 'But how can I do that?' Well, let me explain it to you. Firstly, comprehend that most of your problems are just a figment of your imagination, they have no real existence, and any problem that plagues the mind can certainly be treated. So, firstly, compile a list of your ten principal problems, and then segregate them into three categories. In the first category, include the problems for which you have a solution, or the problems which you can solve. Then, straightaway dive headlong into solving all such problems. Once you have accomplished this, in the second category, list all the problems which even Nature cannot solve; for example, succumbing to a hand injury, your child failing his exams, or facing a loss in business. These are all incidents which have already occurred, but they are still tormenting your mind as an unsolved problem. Now, pray tell me, how can you term something as a problem, when even Nature cannot solve it? For, it is the ultimate law of Nature that anything that has once taken place in this world can never be reversed. Then, what should be done in such a case, you might ask. Why, nothing at all, simply accept it. And let me tell you, the moment you accept it, that problem will become a part of your life; it will become your present-day reality, and hence, it will no longer remain a 'problem'.

To elucidate further on this point, I will narrate a beautiful incident to you to explain how this acceptance can prove to be a resolution to your problem. Once upon a time, there lived a great *fakir* in Turkey, who was quite famed and revered in his community. He had established a one-of-a-kind school wherein innumerable students were benefitting from his knowledge. And as far as his personal life was concerned, he was leading a blissful and contented life with his wife and two children. He loved his children so dearly that even if they came home late from play, he would wait for them and partake of his meal only after they had returned. Likewise, if he was delayed in returning home for some reason, his children too would wait for him to return, and they would then have their supper together.

But, one day, as fate would have it, the children met with an accident, falling into a deep well while playing. As the well was quite deep, neither of the two could be saved. Meanwhile, the *fakir,* who had gone out for the day, returned home late. Having returned from a long journey, he was understandably a little weary and tired. His wife, although disconsolate by the untimely death of their children, had concealed her sorrow and grief, in view of the *fakir's* weariness. She wanted the *fakir* to eat something and gather his strength, before she broke the terrible news to him, so she served him the meal before revealing the ghastly incident about their children. Meanwhile, the *fakir* looked at his wife in astonishment when she laid the table and began serving him food. The children had not returned home yet, and never in his life had he had supper without his children. Then, why was his wife behaving so strangely today? So, he immediately asked her, "My dear! Have I ever partaken of my meal without the children? What then is the reason for serving me my meal, when they have not returned yet?"

Caught in a dilemma, what could the poor wife say! But she had to say something, and she had to handle the situation tactfully. So, she replied, "As it happens, you are exhausted and the children have gone with their friends to the neighbouring village, so there is every possibility of them returning home late. Perhaps, they might even eat something on the way... That is why, I served you your meal, without waiting for them to return."

The *fakir* replied, "True... I am tired but not so much that I cannot wait for the children to return home. And how does it matter if the children have already eaten; at their age, they can certainly eat a full meal again. Regardless of how much they eat on their way back and how late they return, they will definitely eat with me again."

Now, what could the wife say in the face of such reasoning. So, albeit unwillingly, she had to apprise the *fakir* of the tragic accident; she was compelled to relate the utterly distressing incident to her husband as he sat over his meal... But then, the unexpected happened! As soon as he heard the news of their children's untimely death, the *fakir* began to eat his meal. Not a trace of grief or pain reflected on his face over the death of his children, and to his wife's bewilderment, he even polished off the children's share of the meal. Much to the wife's dismay, he did not ask for any details about the children's accident while having his meal or even afterwards. And after finishing the meal, as was his wont, he went for a stroll and after returning, he peacefully lay on his bed and fell into a sound sleep. Hearing her husband sleep soundly despite being apprised of the tragic death of their children, the wife, feeling distraught, lay wide awake, tossing and turning in bed all night; a crushing pain seared through her entire being at her husband's strange behaviour, almost as if someone had stabbed her heart with a thousand daggers! But as soon as the *fakir* woke up in the morning, she confronted him and asked him to reveal the reason behind his undecipherable behaviour. The *fakir* sat her down lovingly beside him and remarked, "Look, my dear! To love, to live with, and to enjoy what one possesses is an art, but to ask about that which is lost, to grieve over it or to mull over it is a malady. Allah had blessed us with those children, and he has taken them back; they were but guests in our life. However, I will admit, for all the time that they graced our lives, we derived great happiness and joy from their very presence. But our happiness does not hinge upon just one blessing of God; he has made us the master of the very art through which we can derive complete enjoyment from whatever we have at any point in time. And even at present, I have you, the school and the children at the school to lend me enjoyment. All I mean to say is, God has bestowed joy and happiness upon me in abundance, and even if I derive full enjoyment from all that he has blessed me with so far, it would suffice a lifetime." Hearing her husband utter such profound words, the wife felt the burden of grief that was tormenting her until this moment ease considerably.

I am sure you must have now comprehended how to put an end to problems by simply accepting them. Now, we come to the third category of problems – the problems for which no immediate solution is available; however, with the passage of time, a remedy to rectify or reverse these problems can surely manifest itself. The nature of these problems is such that they are dangling halfway between the other two categories. So, do not fret, as I have oft-said, obliterate them from your mind, and leave them in Nature's care, till the time a solution does not manifest on its own. To state it simply, entrust such problems to Nature's system of justice, and stop thinking about them altogether. Then, one day, you will either find a solution to such problems, or they will become inevitable and irreversible. At that point in time, if you have found a solution to that problem, resolve it, and if it has become inevitable, accept it as such... what you must comprehend is, either way, that problem has certainly been solved.

I believe, you must have comprehended the workings of this great spiritual science. To summarise the discussion so far, divide your problems into three categories. Solve the problems which you can resolve on your own, accept those which have become inevitable, and forget the ones which do not fit into either of these categories, entrusting them to Nature's system of justice. By adopting this stance, you will straightaway be delivered from all your problems, and this will instantly accrue you two wonderful benefits. One, your energy and enjoyment will increase manifold on account of leading a problem-free life, and second, as you have entrusted all your problems to Nature, you will continue to derive its absolute support and cooperation. To make this task easier for you, I have prepared a chart for you to fill below.

1 **Problem** ....

To solve the above problem,

Tick (✔) any one of the options given below

- [ ] **It can be resolved**
- [ ] **It is inevitable and I have accepted it**
- [ ] **It can be resolved but not right away, hence I have assigned it to Nature's system of justice**

2 **Problem** ....

To solve the above problem,

Tick (✔) any one of the options given below

- [ ] **It can be resolved**
- [ ] **It is inevitable and I have accepted it**
- [ ] **It can be resolved but not right away, hence I have assigned it to Nature's system of justice**

3 Problem ....

....

....

....

....

....

To solve the above problem,

Tick (✔) any one of the options given below

☐ **It can be resolved**

☐ **It is inevitable and I have accepted it**

☐ **It can be resolved but not right away,
hence I have assigned it to Nature's system of justice**

4 Problem ....

....

....

....

....

....

To solve the above problem,

Tick (✔) any one of the options given below

☐ **It can be resolved**

☐ **It is inevitable and I have accepted it**

☐ **It can be resolved but not right away,
hence I have assigned it to Nature's system of justice**

5 **Problem** ....

....

....

....

....

....

To solve the above problem,

Tick (✔) any one of the options given below

- [ ] **It can be resolved**
- [ ] **It is inevitable and I have accepted it**
- [ ] **It can be resolved but not right away,**
  hence I have assigned it to Nature's system of justice

6 **Problem** ....

....

....

....

....

....

To solve the above problem,

Tick (✔) any one of the options given below

- [ ] **It can be resolved**
- [ ] **It is inevitable and I have accepted it**
- [ ] **It can be resolved but not right away,**
  hence I have assigned it to Nature's system of justice

7 **Problem** ....

....

....

....

....

....

To solve the above problem,

Tick (✔) any one of the options given below

- [ ] **It can be resolved**
- [ ] **It is inevitable and I have accepted it**
- [ ] **It can be resolved but not right away, hence I have assigned it to Nature's system of justice**

8 **Problem** ....

....

....

....

....

....

To solve the above problem,

Tick (✔) any one of the options given below

- [ ] **It can be resolved**
- [ ] **It is inevitable and I have accepted it**
- [ ] **It can be resolved but not right away, hence I have assigned it to Nature's system of justice**

9 **Problem** ....

....

....

....

....

....

To solve the above problem,
Tick (✔) any one of the options given below

- [ ] **It can be resolved**
- [ ] **It is inevitable and I have accepted it**
- [ ] **It can be resolved but not right away,**
hence I have assigned it to Nature's system of justice

10 **Problem** ....

....

....

....

....

....

To solve the above problem,
Tick (✔) any one of the options given below

- [ ] **It can be resolved**
- [ ] **It is inevitable and I have accepted it**
- [ ] **It can be resolved but not right away,**
hence I have assigned it to Nature's system of justice

To conclude, include anything which is bothering you in your list of problems and jot it down in the above chart. Once you have noted down your ten principal problems, mark a tick in any of the above three boxes for each of your problems and then strictly adhere to it, with complete honesty. Then, observe whether you are straightaway liberated from all your problems or not. Believe me, you will be liberated! Ergo, undertake the exercise of composing a list of ten key problems every six months or so, and continue to be delivered from all your problems instantly. At the same time, you will attain Nature's support as well to make your path smoother and easier. Come what may, always keep your mind free of problems. Tell me, does it behove you to live a life beset by problems, when you are neither required to make the winds blow nor make the moon and stars shine? Ergo, steer clear of all your problems right here, right now!

7. Follow the Natural Principle to Deal With Problems

After having discussed the various aspects of safeguarding yourself from all the problems afflicting you, let us grasp what truly constitutes a problem. Any problem or predicament that has a solution, or simply put, that which you can solve straightaway can be termed a problem. So, tell me, how can something which cannot be solved be labelled as a problem? The issue that you are terming as a problem is a product of your thoughts, a mark of your feeble mentality. Thus, resolve from this day onwards that you will assuredly not succumb to mental frailties and that you will consider only that matter as a problem, to which a solution is available to you. And a problem that has a solution no longer remains a problem, because you will surely go ahead and resolve it. At the same time, stop considering those matters as problems, for which you have no solution; simply assign them to Nature's system of justice and free yourself from the task of worrying about them. In other words, from this very moment, stop believing that life is afflicted by any problem and straightaway experience the feeling of soaring freely in the sky, with open arms and a beaming smile on your face. This is verily Nature's design for every human being, and also the secret behind the greatness of all great people. Typically, many people feel that the great personalities who have walked this earth have led a life of struggles and troubles, but the fact is, they simply did not deem their troubles as troubles. In fact, they always lived a merry and carefree life, entrusting all their difficulties to Nature. But when you peek into their lives, all you can see are trials and tribulations; your myopic vision fails to discern their light-heartedness because of your lack of psychological knowledge. Ergo, if you wish to attain greatness, assign your troubles to Nature and start living a peaceful and merry life. And rest assured, Nature will take care of the rest for you.

The fact that I am stating here is backed by a great spiritual science. Firstly, do not presume that you are living all alone. This world is home to more than seven billion human beings, and millions of events are occurring in the blink of an eye, at every moment, in accordance with Nature's system of justice. Now, you possess absolutely no knowledge of why and for whom these events are taking place, and because of your small-mindedness and blinkered outlook, you feel that all the unfortunate events are occurring only to besiege you and rob you of your happiness. But in reality, this is not the case. The greater majority of events are transpiring to assail somebody else; it is you who are at fault for pointlessly becoming a party to it and turning somebody else's problem into your own. And then, you torture yourself by stressing over that problem for months and years together until eventually, you realise that you had put yourself under so much mental strain for a problem that never materialised. From now on, observe for yourself, the preponderance of your problems do not really exist, but you torment yourself with worry for no good reason. In other words, even though the problem exists in your mind, it has no existence in reality. The point that demands your attention here is, if you remain besieged by problems in your head and persist with subjecting yourself to mental anguish, then you will fritter away your entire life in (harbouring) mental stress and tension. In that case, how will you ever be able to lead a fruitful and productive life, forget about attaining greatness?

Thus, imbibe this ultimate principle of Nature once and for all. Nature has no intention of unleashing problems on humankind, and you certainly have the solution to the problems strewn in your path by Nature. Ergo, henceforth, do not deem something which has no solution as a problem. Pass a firm resolution and entrust that so-called problem to Nature; and Nature will convey the problem to the person it belongs to. Stop troubling and tormenting yourself over it unnecessarily. And as soon as you entrust the problem to Nature, a miracle will surely manifest, bringing you immediate deliverance from all worries and tension, while at the same time, most of your problems will simply pass you by. In short, entrust your life completely to Nature, for, there is no other way that will serve your ultimate benefit. And only if you do so, will you be able to lead a life devoid of worries. Ergo, pass a resolution to this end, and henceforth, whenever you sense a problem rearing its head, utilise your resolution as a *Japa Mantra* and entrust that problem to Nature. And if a resolution for the problem is readily available to you, resolve the problem. But regardless of the circumstances you find yourself entrenched in, always remain free of worries and tensions.

Your Resolution

....

....

....

....

....

8. Discern What is Transpiring in Everybody's Mind Effortlessly

You are completely oblivious to the fact that there lies a Collective Conscious Mind within you. And the peculiarity of this mind is, it is connected with the minds of all human beings. Employing the power of this mind, you can grasp what is transpiring within the mind of any person, whom you are on close terms with. All you need to do is, sit in solitude and contemplate over the person whose mind you want to probe; you must become so profoundly engrossed in contemplation about that person that you become oblivious to your own existence. By employing this method, you will immediately discern what lies within that person's heart; you will apprehend how much positivity or negativity he harbours for you. In other words, you will catch his frequency. And let me tell you, many a time, you do catch other people's frequency. Ergo, with the aid of this application, grasp the frequency of any person at any time, and you can do so without even stepping out of your house. Then, it is irrelevant if decades have passed by since you last met that person or that he stays thousands of miles away from you today. Such concerns are no barrier to your Collective Conscious Mind. But you must ensure that 'you' do not intervene in this application, your former memories or your personal opinion concerning that person should not cloud your mind; only then will you succeed in catching the frequency of that person. Besides, in this world we are living in, it hardly takes a second for a friend to turn into a foe and vice versa. That being the case, to arrive at a decision about any person today based on his past behaviour is nothing but rank foolishness. Here, you must also comprehend that with the aid of this application, you can catch the frequency of only that person whom you know well. Furthermore, you can only catch his frequency, and nothing else. You can also term this as telepathy, which is nothing but a wireless communication between two people. You must have surely heard of instances where a mother feels her heart thud with trepidation about her child being in dire straits, although the child is living miles away from her. This fine-tuning between two individuals is quite easy, and wireless communication is, indeed, accurate. Ergo, it is high time you learn to utilise it, because your life will become much simpler than before, simply with the knowledge of what is transpiring in the other person's mind.

9. Kindle Positivity in Other People's Minds for You

Needless to say, when you can become privy to the frequency of the other person's mind through your Collective Conscious Mind, then you can indubitably change that frequency as well. And as both these tasks occur through the means of the Collective Conscious Mind, the method employed for both is also similar; there is no separate practical application for this purpose. Be it your boss or your lover, you can kindle positivity for yourself in their minds, sitting in the comfort of your home. To do so, you must sit in solitude and become absorbed in thoughts of that person once again. Close your eyes and become intent on continually harbouring positive thoughts about that person. Upon doing so continuously, positive feelings will begin to kindle in the other person's heart for you. But yes, this contemplation should take place at a profound level and with absolute perfection. While contemplating, one should become completely absorbed in the other person to the exclusion of everything else, even forgetting one's own existence. And now that you are in the final phase of this book, by this point, I'm sure you must have comprehended the depths of spiritual science to a considerable extent. Hence, it is needless to explain every practical application at length. I hope, you must have grasped this practical application sincerely and completely, and I am also sanguine that you will derive optimum benefit from this useful application. This is an application for which you need not pass any resolution, because this is a method in itself.

10. Be the Master of Your Universe One Day at a Time

You believe that your life belongs to you and its complete responsibility has been thrust upon your shoulders. But in point of fact, this thinking is far removed from the truth. Your life is verily Nature's responsibility; the fault lies with you for not entrusting that responsibility to it. However, the time has come for you to realise that you need to entrust your life to Nature, for therein lies your ultimate benefit. Having said that, let me provide you an extremely simple practical application that will help you do so; every day, when you wake up, resolve that, 'This day belongs to me, while the rest of my days are Nature's. Ergo, I will shoulder the responsibility of this day myself.' And thereafter, plan all the tasks that are urgent in conjunction with your home, work, relaxation, friends, and so on, and undertake them in the best possible manner. Deal with all your daily duties, and live the day performing all the tasks your mind concurs with. Simply resolve that, 'I am the master of this day, and I will spend it in the best possible way, in every sense of the word.' Then, stop right at that point; do not concern yourself the least bit with the rest of your life. For, that belongs entirely to Nature, not you. If you need to spend some portion of today in making plans for tomorrow, then do so, because after all, that is also a part of your 'today'. Just ensure that you leave its outcome to Nature. In other words, let Nature's system of justice decide whether the outcome it ushers in the future will materialise as per your wishes or not. Do not, under any circumstances, stake your claim over and above today. Simply consider 'today' as your own and plan to spend it in the best possible manner when you wake up each morning and retire to bed in peace at night. Then, the next morning will dawn and you will be bestowed with a fresh, new day. So, consider yourself the master of that day and plan to spend it in the best possible manner once again. In this fashion, with each passing day, you will spend your entire life spectacularly, and upon doing so, you will also continually receive assistance from Nature. And in this manner, Nature will one day ascend you to the pinnacle of success. On your part, embed the belief that you hold the ownership of your life only for the present day; worry about that one day only, and entrust the worry of the rest of your life to Nature. This is a simple and direct method to lead a worry-free, beautiful and successful life. Ergo, pass a firm resolution to this end, and make it your *Japa Mantra* to be recited each morning. And with its help, confine your scope of authority to a single (present) day. Then, every new morning, become the master of a fresh day. Do not concern yourself with how many more mornings you may be granted. Leave everything concerning the future upon Nature, and spend today in the most splendid way. Behold then, the transformation that manifests in your life with each passing day!

....

....

....

....

....

....

....

....

Core Essence of Step 3

To summarise the essence of step 3, the true reins of your life lie in the hands of Nature and to entrust one's life to Nature is called wisdom in the truest sense. This is precisely what all the great people who have left an indelible mark in this world have done, and I am confident that you will also succeed in working this miracle into your life. A word to the wise...to hand over the reins to Nature entails handing them over for good. Thereafter, never again must you be worried about yourself, because the moment you give in to worry, Nature will withdraw its support. For, as long as you remain concerned about yourself, Nature will not worry about you. Remember, even a smidgen of adulteration is not acceptable to Nature. Refuge, complete and absolute, is the only recourse to attain Nature's support, and know that, in the absence of its support, life will remain devoid of joy and success. Ergo, without further ado, surrender your life to Nature; derive the utmost benefit from all the practical applications provided in this book, and lay down the foundation to a life filled with love, beauty and wonder.

Now that you have comprehended this vital fact, apprehend another crucial point of spiritual psychology. For, if there is one matter regarding which the whole of humankind is well and truly confounded, it is verily religion. Hence, let me make it absolutely clear, do not commit the grave mistake of deeming your communities or their scriptures as religion. The greater part of humankind has blundered as far as religion is concerned, and consequently, the lives of majority of human beings are wasted in bearing the hard knocks of life. Ergo, grasp once and for all that religion is nothing but Nature's creation, and the sole objective of religion is to effect the betterment and advancement of human beings, which in turn, is conceivable only within the bounds of Nature. This begets the logical question, who is a theist? Well, according to Nature's perception, only a person who has established a connection between his powerful minds and Nature is a theist. Viewed from this perspective, the only goal of this book is to turn you into a true theist. This, in turn, raises the question, who are the people who spend their lives placing their faith in religious places and religious scriptures? For, in common parlance, it is only such people who are termed theists. So, in this context, let me share with you an observation of Swami Vivekananda. Providing the perfect definition of a theist, he had stated...the one who lives relying upon himself is a theist, while the one who spends his life placing his faith in somebody else is an atheist. In other words, the ones who spend their lives placing their faith in places of worship and religious scriptures are also nothing but atheists if considered in the truest sense of the term, and that is precisely why, their lives are languishing in such a desolate state. Ergo, if you wish to set your life on the path of progress, you have no recourse except becoming a true theist by accepting Nature's refuge. And becoming a true theist is possible only when you sever all external connections, or in other words, when you become a true atheist. If you carefully consider, you will discern that the objective of steps 1 and 2 is verily to turn you into a true atheist, to teach you to assume your responsibility yourself, and to sever connections with all external support and refuges. Basically, the aim of steps 1 and 2 is to help you sever all bondages and become completely independent. At the same time, these steps are designed to initially make you engage in trials and efforts and battle the odds. And when you realise that nothing of consequence is happening with your efforts, you will comprehend the significance of Nature's ultimate authority. And only then, will you be able to become a true theist, by accepting Nature's refuge.

If understood in totality, most people are so-called theists and such people are entirely disconnected from Nature; this is the reason why their lives are in such a pitiable state. But the question is, how will the lives of such people take a turn for the better? The fact of the matter is, one shall attain greatness only by surrendering to Nature. But at the same time, it is also true that a person who goes about his life placing his faith in thousands of mortals cannot straightaway begin to lead a life relying solely upon Nature. Therefore, he will first have to rid himself of his multiple dependencies and only then will he be able to place his trust in Nature. If grasped from this perspective, this is a comprehensive book, which in steps 1 and 2, turns a so-called theist into a true atheist, and thereafter, it shapes him into a true theist in step 3. For, the principle of spiritual science is simple and straightforward—a so-called theist can never become a true theist, without first becoming an atheist. That is precisely why, majority of the great beings of the world are either atheists or true theists. I believe you must have now apprehended this entire science, and the subject of religion must have also become crystal clear to you. Therefore, I hereby extend my best wishes to you for a wonderful life abounding in good health, cheer and joy, and on this pleasant note, I herewith lay my pen to rest.